CANNING AND PRESERVING FOOD FOR BEGINNERS

The Complete Guide to store everything in jars (canned meat, jams, vegetables, jellies, pickles) - homemade recipes for pressure canning, and Fermenting

---

© written by : Elisa Dayson

Table of Contents

Introduction   **8**
  Canning for Good Health 9

  Finding your Produce 10

Chapter 1 : Canning History 17

Chapter 2: Benefits of canning 25

  Main Reasons that People Start Canning and Preserving 31

    Many People Prefer the Taste and Quality That Comes With Canning & Preserving Your Food: . 32

    Canning and Preserving Your Own Food will Make Great Gifts Later On: 33

    Canning is a Hobby That Can Give Personal Satisfaction and a Sense of Peace: 34

    Canning & Preserving Your Food is Helpful When You Grow It on Your Own: 35

    Canning & Preserving Your Food Will Help You Financially: 35

    Canning & Preserving Food Can Be Very Eco-Friendly When Done Right: 36

    If You Can & Preserve Your Food It Is Often Healthier: 36

Chapter 3 : Principles of Food Preservation 37

How to Prevent or Slow Down Food Spoilage 37

How to Preserve Food 40

Popular Ingredients Used in Canning 44

The Two Methods for Home Canning 48

Pickling and Fermenting 57

    Choosing the best quality produce for canning 59

    Tips to avoid spoilage, and pitfalls to avoid 60

Chapter 4 : Canning and Preserving Safety Tips 65

Choose the Right Canner 65

Opt for a Screw Top Lid System 66

Check Your Jars, Lids and Bands 67

Check for Recent Canning Updates 68

Pick the Best Ingredients 69

Clean Everything 70

Follow Your Recipe 70

Cool the Jars 71

Don't Risk It 71

How to Prepare Healthy Canned Foods 72

Canning without Using Sugar 73

Canning with Less Salt 73

Canning Baby Foods 74

Where To Store 74

How to store canned food 75

How much to store canned food 76

How long to store open canned food 77

Chapter 5 : Recipes 78

    Stewed Tomatoes 78

    Corn - Whole Kernel 79

    White Potatoes - Cubed or Whole 80

    Pickled Beets 82

    Marinated Fava Beans 83

    Tomatoes - Whole 85

    Spiced Beets 87

    Spicy Green Beans 89

    Damson Jellies 91

    Grape Jelly 93

    Guava Jelly 95

    Strawberry Jellies 97

    Apple Jelly 98

    Corn Cob Jelly 101

    Jalapeno Jelly 103

    Dandelion Jelly 105

    Orange Jelly 106

    Garlic Jelly 108

    Mint Jelly 110

    Cherry Jelly 112

Mango Jelly	113
Ginger Jelly	115
Hot Jelly	116
Mango Jams	118
Strawberry Jam	120
Peach Jam	121
Blueberry Jam	122
Peach Jam	124
Tomato Jam	126
Orange Jam	128
Fig Jam	129
Cherry Jam with Sour Taste	131
Apple Jam	132
Almond and Cherry Jam	134
Jalapeno Jam	136
Pear Jam	137
Mixed Fruit Jam	139
Kiwi Jam	140
Double Berry Jelly	142
Blueberry Jam	144
Lemon Strawberry Marmalade	146
Salsa Verde	148
Spicy Pineapple Salsa	150

Zesty Tomato Salsa	152
Tropical Fruit Salsa	154
Sweet Plum Chutney	156
Apricot Pear Chutney	158
Lime Jelly	160
Pickled Peaches	162
Tomato Salsa	166
Fig Jam	169
Ginger Nectarine Jam	172
Blackberry & Apple Jam	174
Raspberry Jam	177
Rosehip Jam	180
Amazing Pear Mincemeat	183
Carrots Canning	186
Tasty Red Pepper	188
Healthy Grape Jelly	191
Canned Chicken	193
Mexican Turkey Soup	194
Fish	195
Cabbage Soup	197
Beef Stew	200
Potato and Leek Soup	203
Veggie Soup	204

Fennel & Carrot Soup 206

Tomato Soup 208

Chicken Soup 210

Home-style Spaghetti Sauce 212

Tomato Soup with Celery 214

Carrot, Coriander, and Ginger Soup 216

Singapore Pepper Sauce 219

Green Lima Vegetable Soup 221

Cabbage and Corned Beef Soup 223

Chicken Broth with Chile and Corn 225

Tasty Beef & Vegetables 228

Mexican Chicken Soup 231

Chapter 6: Frequently asked questions 234

Chapter 7: Some Other Food Preservation Techniques
.... 240

Conclusion 244

Introduction

Food preservation has become a necessary endeavor in today's food industry from the sheer diversity and variety of food that is on offer. The waste that occurs in modern consumption methods is unprecedented now – smaller families, mean that there is more food than they're able to consume and food spoilage encompasses the leftovers. Learning to preserve food is therefore a way to reduce wastage as well as save money on buying in excess.

Canning for Good Health

Canning ingredients are also a great way of maintaining a healthy diet. It means firstly, you do not have the issue of having to buy smaller amounts of convenience foods, and your food will last longer for you. Cooking your own food, in principle, is a lot healthier because you know exactly what's going into them. The element of control means you can extol a healthier and less fat ridden diet.

Also, when preserving food, there is emphasis on getting rid of the fat. Trimming the fat from meats, removing any excess oil etc. Fat and preservation are not two concepts that work in tandem with each other so this is good news for a calorie-controlled diet.

The worst thing about healthy eating and losing weight is that food without the fat lacks flavor – or that's the fear anyhow. Preservation methods use ingredients that really lock in flavor and bring pungent and intense notes to typically healthy food like vegetables, which will enhance your meal without adding calories.

All of the recipes in this book can be attempted in a low fat way. As well as low sodium and low sugar suggestions, replace pectin with a sugar free version, reduce salt levels and use more acidic substances. Canning is definitely something you want to get into for a more weight-controlled lifestyle.

Finding your Produce

If the aim of canning and preservation is to remain healthy, save money and reduce waste, then you'll want to firstly find the best quality produce. While one of the goals of preserving food is to reduce waste, that's not to say your thinking in this process starts when food is on the way out or just before it expires. Unfortunately it doesn't work like that. Food that's already old and getting a little spoilt, although not completely off, will not taste particularly great and will not last that long in any case.

Vegetables should always be fresh and crisp. Avoid those with deteriorating outer layers, or brown spots. These should always be removed if you do use vegetables like this.

Fruit needs to be ripe, softened fruit will start to mush when you put it through the preservation process or start to cook with them to make the various recipes.

Meat, poultry and other animal products need to be fresh and kept refrigerated until being used. Fat is not welcome in the preservation process and all the fat needs to be removed.

Preservation and canning is a process that's great to use if you find some great bulk buys or if you know early on that you won't need all of your produce. Markets are excellent for these types of deals. Better yet, pick some at the allotments or pick your own farms and if you're feeling particularly committed, start to grow your own produce, then you know exactly how your produce has been treated and what's going into your body. That's when you'll find these preservation techniques really useful.

Equipment

Canning and preserving will work to save you money in the long run and is definitely for the frugal minded consumer and domesticant.

However, there is a certain amount of investment that you'll need to make prior to initiating the canning process.

Basic Utensils

Firstly, you'll need some basic utensils and kitchen equipment

- Several sizes of saucepans, medium and large in particular.

- A crock pot or large pot, in order to cook large quantities.

- The use of a frying pan, skillet and oven.

- Wooden spoons, plastic spatula and forks.

- Potato masher

- Food processor.

- Sharp knife.

- Chopping board.
- Several mixing bowls.
- Long tongs.
- Sieve.
- Colander.
- Strainer.
- Ladel.
- Funnel.

Specialist Equipment

In order to preserve and can on a long-term basis, some specialist equipment will be needed.

- **Dehydrator.** If you are planning on drying food (see later segment on drying), you will need a dehydrator. While you can use an oven, or a dry stillroom, dehydrators are by far the most efficient method of drying food. It is simply an electrical appliance that has a heat element and a fan element. You can buy them quite easily on the internet or through catalogue or mail order shops and department stores. Try and find one made of metal or high grade plastic with a timer and temperature regulator. They vary in terms of which way the air flows too, horizontally or vertically. Horizontal flow dehydrators allow different foods to be dried at one time.

- **Jars.** Jars are the staple of the canning process and you'll want several types of sizes depending on the quantities you produce and also what you're canning, they can vary quite a lot. The glass jar is reusable. With the jars come lids and bands. The lids have a sealing compound and the bands are placed around the lids. The lids and bands are required if you are canning for long periods of time.

- **Water Bath Canner.** A water bath is a large heavyset pot with a rack at the bottom, which is used for canning certain types of preserves, those with high acid content. A special water bath canner has the advantage of including a heavyset lid that seals. However, you can use a large pot with a rack that fits in if you prefer.

- **Pressure Canner.** A pressure canner should always be used for low acid foods. This is a large, usually aluminum pot that includes a pressure gauge and rack. This is the only safe method for canning low acid foods if you wish to preserve them for long

periods of time.

Image Credit: All American

The idea of food preservation and canning may seem like a daunting task but this book will go through simple step-by-step procedure. It will give you the theory behind food preservation so you fully understand what happens to food and why and will provide you with easy recipes using every day ingredients that often go to waste.

This book should make anyone with a kitchen, a proficient preserver and canner.

Chapter 1 : Canning History

There has been a need for food preservation for as long as the people have. But it has not always been as foolproof as today's choices. To be sure, the road toward developing healthy, reliable food preservation methods is fraught with illness, useless food, and even death. Fortunately, we are able to harvest the experience that has been gained in the past. And if we use this information wisely, we will be able to avoid repeating those errors.

The bulk of our world's regions cannot be harvested year-round. Even if your preferred prey is available, it isn't prudent to hunt all year. So, how do we feed into the "off-season?" We have to prepare for these times, as they most certainly will come. Food planning became more than just going up the hill to see if the berry bushes were still ripe.

Humans also built ways of preserving food over time.

Dehydration was noticed, and the moisture content of meats, fruits, herbs, and vegetables was reduced. This humidity was, in part, the rotting cause of these foods. The easiest form of food preservation was thinly sliced and hanged or spread out to dry in the sun.

Followed by salting, brining, and smoking. All of these approaches were cheap and convenient enough for every household to be able to cater to their own needs.

Bacteria and enzymes were discovered as science progressed, and their effects on food were discovered; prevention was learned. When food was brought up to a certain temperature and then sealed in containers resistant to air and moisture, eliminating any air in the container during the process, it could be stored for long periods. "Canning" was invented, as this practice was known.

Following World War II, as the electrical grid reached even the furthest outlying farms and ranches, and with the rise in industrialization, prices for various metals dropped, freezing food became a reliable method of food conservation.

Although the most labor-intensive approach is the canning process, all methods foster a sense of pride, accomplishment, and self-reliance. There's nothing like opening the pantry or freezer door on a cold winter's day, where the snow – already up to the sills of the window – falls down so hard that you can't see your mailbox, finding row after row of cleanly labeled goods and meats, and realizing once again that if the world ended outside your house, your family would still eat well.

Definition of preservation methods

Canning- Cooking food for storage in airtight containers. This process uses aluminum, tin, or glass containers. Hot food is packed into the container and sealed under pressure or under a bath of boiling water.

Dehydration-Simply put, for preservation, remove water from food items. Food was thinly sliced in early history and put into the sun to dry on flat rocks. Earlier, as people became less nomadic, they installed racks to hang long, thin slices of beef, just think of jerky.

Commercially purchased dehydrators use mesh screens for shelves, and electrical fans to pump air into the food continuously. The mesh screens allow both sides of the food to enter the air, while the fan speeds up the process. Bacteria must grow and multiply in humidity. The removal of moisture from food eliminates the bacteria that cause spoilage.

Dry-Salting Dehydrate – This method extracts moisture from food and requires a lot of salt. This moisture dissolves the salt into a brine, which inhibits micro-organisms' growth. That way, only small or fine foods can be preserved. Small fish that way are also protected. Finished correctly, then the fish can be refrigerated for up to two years.

Fermentation – Although very similar to brining, fermentation involves very demanding salt, vinegar, and temperature measurements. They convert vegetable sugars into acids, due to benign micro-organisms that interact with salt brine.

This method produces dill pickles, which can take three to six weeks to prepare. These foods may be kept indefinitely if processed (using pressure canning) after the fermentation period.

Freezing – position the protected food in an environment which keeps it at 0oF [-18oC]. This way of preserving food is the easiest. It also contains the bulk of foods nearest to their original type. Freezing is a very economical way of preserving food, not including the original investment in the actual appliance. A fast blanch to halt enzyme development, and protection from the frigid, dry air is all that is needed in preparation.

Jelling – Preserving with sugar appears to be a contradiction in terms. It is true that micro-organisms thrive on a weak sugar solution. In a strong concentration, sugar has a dehydrating effect, similar to that of salt, inhibiting the development of micro-organisms.

Once pectin is added, gels or jellies are retained to the fruit. Jellies, jams, marmalades, and preserves are all made from the same operation. They are then sealed with paraffin in sterile containers and stored in a cold, dry environment. Only fruit butter, cheeses, and preserves of whole pieces of fruit should be processed in a water bath instead.

Irradiation – Though not accessible to the in-house food preserver, this preservation process is being used more often as the technology is improving. Eating is subject to a dose of ionizing radiation in its simplest sense.

The dosage of the radiation and the exposure period differ. This process works by damaging the DNA of the microbe so that it cannot repair it. The microbe cannot grow when this happens, nor can it conduct cell division, its reproductive system. The microbe is destroyed outright if the dose is high enough.

While the food itself cannot become radioactive (particles transmitting the radiation are not radioactive themselves), and this food preservation technique is used in more than fifty countries around the world because of its connection with the nuclear industry, some people in the US still consider food irradiation controversial.

Pickling- This process, also called brining, infuses wonderful flavors into the preserved food. Brine is produced, which typically contains salt, sugar, and vinegar. The brine is combined with herbs or other flavoring ingredients and then heated.

The food that is being processed is then dipped into the brine. Ice can be used to avoid any fermentation. Brining periods can be as short as fifteen minutes or as long as months depending on the food being processed and the amount of flavor to be infused.

Smoking – Smoking often depletes it from moisture in the same way as dehydration protects meats. The meat, therefore, retains the scent of wood smoke, flavoring it in a way that cannot be duplicated elsewhere.

The choice of wood is a great consideration for the desired end product, from the softly scented maple wood to the heady flavors derived from oak or hickory smoke. Smoking times can vary from a few hours or more to a week. This way, preserved meats do need refrigeration. Smoking can also be used for salting or brining purposes.

Chapter 2: Benefits of canning

Home canning and preserving are one of the methods to protect your food from spoilage. Although modern refrigeration technology allows us to keep our foods fresh for a few weeks, canning and preserving can help increase the lifespan of food longer than refrigeration. Moreover, canned foods do not rely on electricity so they don't spoil even if you have an emergency power blackout for two days. If you haven't started canning then now is the time that you should. Below are the benefits of canning that will convince you to start today.

- *Convenience:* Canning allows you to build a pantry full of homemade foods that can fit in your busy lifestyle.

- *Steady supply of homegrown foods:* Although you can buy factory canned fruits and vegetables from your local grocery stores, you really don't have any idea of the kinds of ingredients that they put in the preserved foods. If you do home canning, you have a stock of fresh and homegrown foods that are not only delicious but also healthy.

- *Savings on food costs:* The purpose of home canning and preserving is to help you save on food costs. Since you take advantage of fresh food when they are in abundance, you end up saving a lot on your food costs.

- *Home canning is a fun activity to do:* Home canning is a chore that the entire family can enjoy. You can do home canning to teach other members of the family on how to be sustainable and not depend too much on store-bought foods.

- *Achieve a sense of fulfillment:* People who home can find sense of fulfillment knowing that they are serving their families foods that you know are healthy.

- *You are in control:* Home canning and preserving requires you to use natural preservatives such as vinegar, sugar and salt. But since you are doing the canning yourself, you can control the amount of sugar, salt and vinegar that you use to preserve your food. Unlike store-bought canned foods, you do not have any idea how much sugar or salt they use to preserve food.

There are many benefits of canning your own food. You benefit from having more food choices, stable supply in your pantry and good overall health for the family. Having said this, it is important that you learn this very important skill so that your entire household can benefit from it.

When you're thinking about canning, you'll want to can things like:

- Fruits
- Vegetables
- Fruit Juices
- Pickles
- Jams
- Relishes

- Condiments
- Jellies
- Vinegars
- Salsas
- Chutneys
- Poultry
- Meat
- Fish

Foods that You ***Cannot*** Can

There are some foods that you will not be able to can such as:

- Flour products, whey, and oats
- Dairy Soy, and Fats
- Thickeners
- Mashed Veggies
- High-Fat Meats

- Candies

These ingredients tend to not work well with the canning process and can go bad inside of the can.

The Equipment for Canning

Canner:

While this will depend on what you are canning, but you will likely require some sort of canner, whether it is a pressure canner or a water-bath canner.

Jars:

Use jars that are specifically made for canning. Others might not seal as well or work with the canning process.

Screw Bands:

The screw bands secure the lids during the canning process.

Jar Lifters:

You'll need something to help you handle the jars during the process as they are often hot during the process.

Clean Cloth:

You'll need something to clean the edges of the jars before you seal them.

Timer:

This will help you when you are trying to track how long the jars have been in the canner.

Flat Rubber Spatula:

This spatula will allow you to remove any air bubbles that are present in the jar before you seal it.

Funnel:

A funnel can be useful if you are trying to get brine into a jar that has a particularly narrow mouth.

Water-Bath Canning vs. Pressure Canning

Water-Bath Canning is a process that uses boiling hot water. The cans, full of the ingredients, are submerged into the boiling water for a certain amount of time according to the recipe. The time period extends when the water temperature is lower.

Pressure canning uses a specific tool that puts the cans under pressure for a period of time. The pressure method can take quite a bit of time.

Foods that Work with Water-Bath Canning

You'll find that some foods work better with the water-bath method. In particular, foods that are acidic will do best here. So use this method for fruit, juices, pickles, jams, relishes, condiments, jellies, vinegars, salsas, and chutneys.

Foods that Work with Pressure Canning

Foods that are less acidic will do a lot better with pressure canning. This means that vegetables, poultry, meat, and fish will do best with this method.

This book contains many different canning recipes that you can try out. They'll help you keep some delicious foods around your house all year long.

Main Reasons that People Start Canning and Preserving

When just beginning, many people do not understand why they should start canning and preserving food, but it's pretty simple. Everyone will of course have their own reasons, but you will find the main reasons below. It'll help you to know why you may want to start canning and preserving your food, and all the benefits that come with it. Of course, despite the benefits and reasons some people start canning and preserving as a hobby that will let them see their work when they're done. Whatever reason you choose is completely up to you.

Many People Prefer the Taste and Quality That Comes With Canning & Preserving Your Food:

Of course, canning and preserving food will change the taste of it, but they sell canned and preserved food in the grocery store as well. Though, the taste of canned and preserved food that you buy from a store is different than the taste of canned and preserve food that you get when you do it yourself. This is because you can control the quality of everything that goes into your canning and preserved food, and usually it is a lot less old by the time you use it if you are canning or even preserving the food yourself.

It isn't a delusion that it tastes better either. Though, putting hard work into it always makes it taste a little more satisfactory than other ways. It's because the product has been harvested at the right time and is locally grown. That is the main reason that it tastes differently when you can and preserve it yourself. It also ensures that you are dealing with a better quality than if you bought it from the store. It all depends on the effort you put into it.

Canning and Preserving Your Own Food will Make Great Gifts Later On:

A main reason that many people overlook to can different foods and preserve them is because it will make wonderful and thoughtful gifts once you're done. This is where you can get creative with what you decide to preserve and can because unique gifts and homemade gifts are wonderful to both receive and give. They also make people feel as if you've truly thought about the gift before you gave it to them. Another wonderful thing about making your own gifts is that you can personalize to a particular theme or person. A pantry full of these homemade preserved and canned foods make a perfect backup for anyone that is on the list.

Canning is a Hobby That Can Give Personal Satisfaction and a Sense of Peace:

There aren't many things that can make you feel satisfied or at peace. It's easy to feel that you've messed up on various things, but a hobby that you can do from start to finish can really help make sure that you feel a sense of satisfaction from it. Of course, you will also find that since you can finish it from the beginning to the end, you'll also feel at peace. It takes a bit of patience, but once you have that mastered it's all the better. The love for canning and preserving food spreads to almost anyone who tries it, and it helps you tell if canning and preserving food is for you. There are blogs and websites dedicated to it, and you'll find many books on the subject as well. It's sometimes nice to have something that you can dedicate your time to, and it helps you to forget about any other worries.

Canning & Preserving Your Food is Helpful When You Grow It on Your Own:

If one of your hobbies is growing your own food from a full garden to a single fruit tree, you will that preserving and canning that home grown food is helpful. You've put your all into growing that food, and more often than not you won't be able to eat it or all or you will get tired of it before you do. Preserving and canning your food makes sure that you put it to good use before it can go to waste, and that helps with a personal satisfaction as well. You don't want anything to go to waste from a personal harvest.

Canning & Preserving Your Food Will Help You Financially:

It's considered to be a normal expensive in our grocery budget, but preserved and canned food can still be draining on our finances. Of course, it is usually best to do that when you are having issues with buying food, even if it is just to make sure that you have enough to make baked goods. It's cheaper to can things when they are in season, and this is the same for any other preservation method. That is the reason that it can help you financially, and you will later have these canned foods and preserved foods for later use, whenever you may need it.

Canning & Preserving Food Can Be Very Eco-Friendly When Done Right:

Canning and preserving food can actually be eco-friendly, and that is the main reason that you want to make sure that you can in the proper way, and this goes for all food preservation. It means the impact on the environment is minimized, unlike when factories do it. Another wonderful thing is that the jars are actually reusable, meaning you're helping the environment even more.

If You Can & Preserve Your Food It Is Often Healthier:

Many people don't know this but preserving your own food and canning it will actually be healthier than the preserved and canned foods that you can buy at the store. That is because they can be BPA free as well as preservative-free, as you can preserve and can food the natural way when you do it yourself. This means that you aren't using harmful pesticides or additives.

Chapter 3 : Principles of Food Preservation

How Does Food Spoil?

The principle behind food preservation boils down to one goal: to prevent food spoilage. Food spoilage is the process by which the quality and edibility of food is deteriorated or its suitability for human consumption is reduced and can lead to it eventually being poisonous and affecting the health of the body.

How to Prevent or Slow Down Food Spoilage

The idea behind preservation is therefore, to inhibit those factors that lead to the spoilage of food. There are four main principles to this:

☐ Prevention of microorganisms

This process is also known as asepsis. In its most natural form, foods are protected by their natural protective shields such as nutshells, the skin on chicken and meat and fruit/vegetable peel. We can also provide protective covering to many of these foods through packaging: clingfilm, canning, polythene bags or foil are some examples by which the average household protects their food from the decomposition caused by microorganisms.

☐ The removal or inactivation of microorganisms

This assumes that there is no protective covering to food already and so any that exist on the food can be killed through a number of methods that ensures the microorganisms cannot survive. This includes the complete removal of moisture (microorganisms cannot thrive without moisture) through drying for example, lowering the temperature to that which they cannot survive (ice can be used for example); increasing the temperature by boiling; increasing sugar/salt content to uninhabitable levels; and removing air; acid and other chemicals (e.g. sodium benzoate and potassium metabi-sulphit); and smoking techniques. Ionized radiation could also be used, although perhaps less common, which involves gamma rays or high-speed electrons. Liquids are often preserved by using the method of filtration to these ends. Filtration can be applied to any clear liquid including water, juices and even alcoholic drinks like beer and wine.

☐ Inactivating enzymes

Enzymes are large molecules that act as catalysts particularly in contact with oxygen and cause the chemical reactions that lead to food spoilage. Many enzymes are naturally present in food, for instance catalase and peroxidase cause the darkening that occurs in diced vegetables and fruits. However, they can be made inactive, the most commonly cited method to do this is by blanching, which means boiling them in water for several minutes. Other ways include, removing oxygen or the use of chemicals and acids. Both plant and animal based foods contain enzymes and they tend to be most active when left at room temperature but this process increases the warmer it gets, which is why food spoilage is more prolific in hotter climates. The oxidation that occurs due to enzymes can be responsible for fats in food turning rancid, a loss of ascorbic acid, the softening of foods and a change in color and texture. The nutrition value ultimately goes down as well and bacteria can start to grow.

- The prevention of damage caused by insects or rodents

This is ultimately done by again protecting the food to ensure that such organisms cannot reach the food, particularly pertinent when transporting food products. Therefore, the elements that prevent this type of spoilage revolve around good packaging, fast transportation or transference of goods and prevention of decomposition, which will involve the three factors above.

How to Preserve Food

There are numerous ways you can preserve food using the principles above. Here are 10 of the most popular and traditional ways:

1. Refrigeration

Cooling food down slows down the rate at which microorganisms grow and reproduce and also slows down the oxidizing activity of enzymes. This is the most common go-to method that preserves food in the short-term and is used by virtually all households in modern times.

2. Drying

While refrigeration is the most common form of food preservation, drying is the oldest. Drying works to disrupt decomposition that occurs from microorganisms. This can be done as naturally as in the sun and many fruits and vegetables can be dried in this manner: sun-dried tomatoes for instance are very popular to this day. This can also be done in less sunny climates in environments where heat is purposefully generated.

3. Freezing

One step above refrigeration is freezing, which is also a common everyday household technique that enables food to be kept for longer. If refrigeration is slowing down the growth of microorganisms then freezing is magnifying this process. It is particularly useful to prolong the quality of foods that have been prepared or cooked already, but perhaps in their original forms they may not have required the freezing process. For example, potatoes do not require freezing to preserve them but cooked into a rosti or waffle, they would do.

4. Heating

Heating food works to kill microorganisms. Many foods are heated before stored to enable their longevity, for example, milk.

5. Salt

Salting is a process that is used to take out moisture and thereby creating an environment on the food's surface where microorganisms cannot grow. It's also known as curing, which can be done with sugar also. Sodium nitrate is also typically used in this process.

6. Sugar

Sugar is a preservative and has typically been used to preserve fruit. Similar to salt, it draws moisture away so microorganisms cannot thrive. It is typically used in a syrup form and fruit is allowed to sit in it, keeping it for longer, particularly peeled fruit, or the fruit can be heated with the sugar.

7. Smoking

Smoking is a technique that was common in the Scandinavian countries. It is typically done using wood and works to depositing pyrolysis products onto the food, which are compounds that dry out the food, hence preserving it. This is typically done to spices, cheeses and certain meats. The

smoked flavor that emerges is also quite popular.

8. Pickling

Pickling involves placing food in a liquid that will kill or inhibit the growth of micro-organisms. Pickling includes chemical pickling and fermentation pickling. Chemical pickling involves placing products in a liquid, always edible, that will kill the organisms. They can include brine i.e. salt water, vegetable oil, alcohol or vinegar. It can also involve boiling the food with the liquid in order to saturate the food with the preserving agent such as with popular salt beef/ corned beef. Fermentation pickling goes off the principle that the food itself contains a preserving agent, lactic acid, which is released. Sauerkraut is often pickled in this manner.

9. Jellying

Jellying is the process of preserving food in a gel like substance that inhibits the growth of microorganisms and takes away oxygen to a degree. This is either done naturally because some foods form a natural gel e.g. eels – jellied eels or using a jellying agent such as gelatin. While jellied eels were popular in the east end of London, there are few naturally jellied foods that are eaten today and the latter method tends to be used when talking about jellying for food preservation.

10. Canning

Canning is the most popular way by which food is preserved, both industrially and in the home. It usually involves cooking food then sealing it in airtight containers so as not to let in oxygen.

Popular Ingredients Used in Canning

Canning is a bit of both art and science. For the best results, it's critical to adhere to recipes as written. Once you master the basics, then you can put your creative talents to work. Ingredients are one key to successful canning. Using the proper ingredients called for in recipes increases the likelihood of success and ensures your food's safety.

Vinegar

The recipes in DIY Canning call for several types of vinegar. Whichever kind you use, it is important that it is 5 percent acetic acid. The amount of acid in vinegar is included on the label. Check the label, as not all vinegars are the same. Because their acidity can vary widely, do not use homemade vinegars for canning.

Note: Do not decrease the amount of vinegar in any recipe. This can lead to a product that is not correctly acidified for safety. Additionally, do not boil vinegar-based pickling liquids beyond the times stated in this book. This can decrease the amount of acetic acid in the mixture. Follow directions closely regarding the boiling of pickling liquid.

Salt

Salt is used in many recipes to add flavor or, as with fermented pickles, aid in the fermentation process. Fine, granulated canning and pickling salt is the best option. This type of salt contains no added fillers to prevent clumping, which can leave an undesirable cloudy haze in your jars of canned foods. Sea salt can also be used when it is pure and contains no fillers. Avoid any colored sea salts.

These can cause undesirable results when pickling. While many people prefer to use kosher salt, heating is often required to dissolve the salt's larger crystals in water (and then the water has to be cooled), adding both time and additional steps to the process. With this in mind, if you don't mind these extra steps, kosher salt can be used. Canning and pickling salt, sea salt, and kosher salt can be found in many grocery stores and specialty stores, or they can be ordered online.

Pectin

Pectin is used in many jam and jelly recipes. This naturally occurring material, found in the greatest quantities in under-ripe fruit, allows the jams and jellies to develop their firm texture. In some recipes, pectin is not used as the fruits have enough natural pectin to make jam easily. Before pectin was commercially made, this is how all jams were made. Pectin is effective in speeding the process and is available in liquid, powder, and low-sugar varieties. Follow the recipe's directions for the type of pectin used, as the methods for using each vary.

Water

When water is needed, you can use filtered water or tap water in most cases. If your tap water tastes good and does not contain a large amount of chlorine or minerals, it is generally fine for the recipes here.

For hard water that leaves deposits in your sinks or toilet, you need to take an extra step to use it. Boil a large pot of water and then let it sit for 24 hours. Remove any scum from the surface and carefully transfer the water to another container, being careful to avoid disturbing the sediment on the bottom.

Chlorine can also be a problem, especially if you are fermenting. If you are using public water, it's a good practice to boil it for two minutes and allow it to cool before using, to eliminate any chlorine.

The Two Methods for Home Canning

So, what does canning really mean?
For those of you who are venturing into this territory for the first time, this is a safe method of preserving food, if done right. This process involves heating food to a certain temperature, capable of killing microorganisms that spoil food, and placing the foods in jars or similar containers to store them. In this heat-driven process, the air is taken out of the jar slowly, and as it cools, a vacuum forms. The vacuum seal simply prevents any microorganisms from entering.

Preparing preserves, jams and jellies at home have become an exciting hobby for millions of people. Also, it is a great way to save bucks and feel independent to make them whenever you need and whenever your mood strikes. Commercially available preserves, jams, relishes, etc. are not only costly as compared to homemade versions, but they are also added with preservatives, additives, artificial colours, and chemicals.

One great advantage of homemade canning is that you can prepare it from fresh ingredients and can ensure that what you are consuming is totally free of additives and preservatives. Another great advantage is that you can keep total control over ingredients quantities; not everyone likes the same amount of sweetness or sourness in preserves and jams. This way, you can adjust sugar quantity as well as savoury ingredients such as vinegar, lemon juice, etc. to suit your taste.

Homemade canning gives you another advantage of preparing them in small quantities; when you prepare them in small quantities, these canning recipes maintain their natural flavours. It takes less space to store and you get to enjoy fresh batches by preparing them at shorter intervals. Short batches provide you with the freedom to make different varieties every time and rotating them as per seasonal ingredients. And if it gets spoiled due to external environmental issues, the wastage amount is quite less.

There are two safe methods of doing this: the water bath and the pressure canning.

The water bath method

This method involves heating food jars by keeping them in boiling water, at a temperature of (212°F at sea level) for a certain period of time. This method is safer for jams, jellies, tomatoes, pickles, and fruits. Foods like tomatoes and figs have a PH level closer to 4.6 and will need added citric acid or even lemon juice while using the water bath method to stabilize PH levels because foods that have a higher PH level than 4.6 can be safely canned with the pressure canning method.

Equipment

For the water bath method, a large cooking pot is used. This has a tight fitting lid on the top, and a wire or wooden rack that keeps your jars from touching each other and possibly cracking and breaking. If you don't have a rack, you can even use some clean dish towels to wrap around your

jars to keep them from bumping into each other and getting damaged.

If you can't find a large cooking pot, any large, metal container that can hold your jars along with 1-2 inches of water covering them, should be good enough. For proper heating of your jars, it's necessary that the diameter of your canner or pot be no more than four inches wider than your stoves burner.

Tips

If you're using an electric range, you canner must have a flat bottom, otherwise your jars won't get proper heating.
Do not use wash kettles that fit over two burners. This will not heat the jars in the middle.
If you're using a solid grate with outdoor fire pits, then you need to ensure that water boils to the right temperature.

The pressure canning method

This method of canning is used for low-acidic foods such as most vegetables (beside tomatoes and pickled vegetables), poultry, fish and sea food, and dairy products. This method involves placing food jars in two to three inches of boiling water in a steam pressure cooker specifically designed for canning. The temperature in a pressure cooker canner reaches 240°F at sea level at a 10 pounds of pressure. The high temperature, above the boiling point of water, which is 212°F, is required to eliminate any chance of bacteria growth in your food. The specific temperature can only be reached through using the pressure cooking method. A major concern for food safety is to prevent and destroy heat-resistant bacteria growth, in particular, the *Clostridium botulinum* which can produce deadly toxins, which can grow really well in low acidic foods like meats and

veggies.

Low acidic foods have a PH level of more than 4.6. Depending on the food and altitude, you're meant to cook the food jars for a specific period of time at the temperature of 240°F or above.

Equipment

For pressure canning, a specially made pot with a heavy lid should be used. The lid should be closed steam-tight. A weighted pressure gauge and a safety fuse are present on the lid to help the pressure build up. The pressure pot will also contain a rack for your jars, and it may or may not contain a gasket.

Pressure cookers for canning usually have a gauge to set per pound of pressure. There are two main types. First, there is the weighted gauge which has three levels of pounds of pressure of 5, 10 and 15 pounds (or 10, 15, 20). The dial gauge measures 0 to 20/25 pounds of pressure.

All pressure pounds must be adjusted according to the altitude of the area where you are canning your food. Please consult the **chart** at the end of this book to adjust to your particular altitude.

Tips

Read the instructions carefully before using it! Safety first.

Canning jars

Using commercial jars like mayonnaise jars or baby food jars is not recommended. Mason jars and Ball jars are specifically designed for home canning and preserving. The jars are the right sizes and are heavy enough to withstand heat and pressure. You can get half-pint, pint, quart, or even half-gallon sized jars. Quart and pint sized Ball jars are most commonly used though. If they are used properly and kept in good condition, they

can be indefinitely reused.

The jar lids come with two-piece, self-sealing lid. This consists of a flat metal disc and a rubber sealing compound at one side around the outer edge and a screw type metal band as well for sealing. The metal band can be reused again and again if it doesn't rust, but the flat lid can be used only once.

Tips

Don't use Atlas jars for preserving and canning.

Don't use jars that have hairline cracks in hopes you can still salvage the jar.

Other canning utensils:

A jar funnel
This will help to pack and pour liquid or other small foods into jars without worry of spillage.

Flat, narrow, rubber spatula

You can use this to remove any trapped air bubbles before sealing your lids.

A lid wand
This is a magnetized wand that can be used to retrieve the treated lids from boiling water.

Jar lifter
This can be used to remove hot jars from boiling pots.

Clean cloths:
You need these to take care of any spillage, wiping the jars and any general cleanup afterwards.

A clock timer
To make sure you're processing time is accurate.

Other utensils like knives, cutting boards, slicers, and peelers, are also used in the canning process to prepare foods for preserving.

Pickling and Fermenting

Pickling is a culinary art that people of different cultures practice all over the globe. To give you an idea what pickled foods look like, examples include, kosher cucumber pickles, salsas, pickled herring, chutneys, kimchi, miso pickles, and others. These examples are found in different countries, and that goes to underline the fact that pickling is a global practice. The big question, really, is what you do in order to be able to say you have pickled your food.

Basically, to make pickles or to pickle your food, what you do is to dip it in a solution that ensures the food has a long shelf life. Salting food is another complementary way of ensuring your food can last long without getting spoilt. In ancient times, nomadic tribes of Africa and elsewhere would salt their meat to ensure it lasts many days and sometimes weeks. In fact, people of different cultures would preserve their food supplies for use during the winter season or during famine, and for that lengthy preservation

they would do salting and pickling.

Sometimes people use vinegar for pickling, and this is because vinegar is acidic enough to kill bacteria that would otherwise cause food to go bad. Other foods are pickled in salt brine, and that is because it is a liquid that enhances fermentation. The reason fermentation is encouraged here is that good bacteria ends up developing, and that makes the food much less vulnerable to the bad bacteria. And, of course, if the growth of bad bacteria is restricted, it means your food cannot get spoilt quickly.

Choosing the best quality produce for canning

Choosing good quality produce ensures that your preserved food lasts longer and tastes excellent every time you eat. These are some tips to choose the best quality produce for best results.

- Fruits and vegetables should be firm and ripe. They should be free of brown spots and mold.

- Greens and leaves should not be discolored or wilted. Use the freshly harvested ones.

- In terms of beans or peas, use dry, mature seeds, and sort out all discolored seeds. Remove any insect-damaged seeds as well.

- With vegetables like carrots or potatoes, they are often just too fibrous. Use smaller carrots and potatoes instead.

- Use brightly colored veggies. They are fresh and give you good results.

- Don't use overripe fruit because their taste and quality as preserves will not improve.

Tips to avoid spoilage, and pitfalls to avoid

When you are completely new to the canning and pickling process, you may make some mistakes that will give you bad canning results. Not to worry! These tips will help you avoid those pitfalls.

- Start with something easy: If you're new to canning, then you need to choose foods which are easy to can to avoid complications in the beginning. Once you've gotten the hang of it, you can progress to more complex ventures with canning and pickling. Try canning tomatoes, or making jam for an easy beginning exercise.

- Choose you food carefully: Make sure your food is free of discoloration and mold, and that produce is freshly harvested and ripe. This will make the canning results spectacular, and the food will last longer.

- Be sure of what canning method to use: Remember that not all foods use the same canning method. You decide which method to use depending on their acidic and pH levels.

- Read the recipe carefully: Get your hands on some current canning recipes. Read them carefully to be sure of the ingredients and that the amounts are correct and up-to-date. Canning recipes and techniques have altered over time, and the more current recipes give you better results.

- Prepare the food properly: If the recipes call for peeling, or cutting the foods, you should follow the recipe exactly and do just that. Remove any stems, pits, and any other parts that are inedible so as to not alter the taste.

- Wash your hands: Make sure that you wash your hands before you prepare the food for canning so that you can avoid any bacteria entering the food.

- Sterilize your jars: Before using the jars, make sure they are properly sterilized after the last usage. You can sterilize your jars by putting them in the dishwasher. Just run them through an entire cycle.

- Leave headspace at the top: When you place food in the jars, pack them tightly, and make sure you leave some space at the top. This can be anywhere from 3mm to 25mm depending on the type of food and what the recipe calls for.

- Add preservatives at the beginning: Before pouring the food into the jar, pour in the preservative, whichever one you may be using, like sugar, citric acid, or honey. You do this so that it mixes in when you pour in the food.

- Air bubbles: Remove any air bubbles at the top by using a flat spatula or a knife and leveling the food, making sure there are no spaces.

- Residues and drips: Wipe down any residues or drips, especially before you seal the jars.

- Check the seal on jars: Check the seals after several hours have passed to make sure the jar contents have pulled down the lids tightly. If you're able to press down the center of a lid, it means the jars haven't been sealed properly.

General tips: When you've opened a jar, refrigerate it, and finish the contents quickly. Also, make labels for your jars, noting the contents and the year. If you've kept many jars, it may be difficult to tell them apart and know what is what.

- Don't use butter or fat while canning unless specifically stated in a recipe, as they don't store that well and may result in food spoilage.

- Don't add thickeners like starches, flours, or even add barley, pasta, or rice to canned foods. After processing, such food can still be unsafe to store. Thickeners absorb liquid and slow down the way food is heated.

- To prevent fruit from darkening, use commercially processed ascorbic acid and sprinkle over fresh, ripe, prepared fruits before canning them. You can even put cut-up fruit in lemon juice. Just drain them before canning.

- Always go for small jars, unless specified otherwise. Larger than recommended jars can result in unsafe food.

Chapter 4 : Canning and Preserving Safety Tips

There are a few safety tips that you should follow when you start canning and preserving foods from home. Canning is a great way to store and preserve foods, but it can be risky if not done correctly. However, if you follow these tips, you will be able to can foods in a safe manner.

Choose the Right Canner

The first step to safe home canning is choosing the right canner. First off, know when to use a pressure canner or a water bath canner. Low acid foods need to be canned using a pressure canner. High acid foods work well in a simple water bath canner but can also be processed in a pressure canner.

Use a pressure canner that is specifically designed for canning and preserving foods. There are several types of canner out there and some are just for cooking food, not for preserving food and processing jars. Be sure that you have the right type of equipment.

Make sure your pressure canner is the right size. If your canner is too small, the jars may be under cooked. Always opt for a larger canner as the pressure on the bigger pots tends to be more accurate, and you will be able to take advantage of the larger size and can more foods at once!

Before you begin canning, check that your pressure canner is in good condition. If your canner has a rubber gasket, it should be flexible and soft. If the rubber is dry or cracked, it should be replaced before you start canning. Be sure your canner is clean and the small vents in the lid are free of debris. Adjust your canner for high altitude processing if needed.

Once you are sure your canner is ready to go and meets all these guidelines, it is time to start canning!

Opt for a Screw Top Lid System

There are many kinds of canning jars that you can choose to purchase. However, the only type of jar that is approved by the USDA is a mason jar with a screw top lid. These are designated "preserving jars" and are considered the safest and most effective option for home preserving use.

Some jars are not thought to be safe for home preserving despite being marketed as canning jars.

Bail Jars, for example have a two-part wire clasp lid with a rubber ring in between the lid and jar. While these were popular in the past, it is now thought that the thick rubber and tightly closed lid does not provide a sufficient seal, leading to a higher potential for botulism. Lightening Jars should not be used for canning as they are simply glass jars with glass lids, with no rubber at all. That will not create a good seal!

Reusing jars from store-bought products is another poor idea. They may look like they're in good condition, but they are typically designed to be processed in a commercial facility. Most store-bought products do not have the two-part band and lid system which is best for home canning. Also, the rubber seal on a store-bought product is likely not reusable once you open the original jar. You can reuse store-bought jars at home for storage but not for canning and preserving.

Check Your Jars, Lids and Bands

As you wash your jars with soapy water, check for any imperfections. Even new jars may have a small chip or crack and need to be discarded. You can reuse jars again and again as long as they are in good condition.

The metal jar rings are also reusable; however, you should only reuse them if they are rust free and undented. If your bands begin to show signs of wear, consider investing in some new ones.

Jar lids need to be new as the sealing compound on the lid can disintegrate over time. When you store your jars in damp places (like in a basement or canning cellar) the lids are even more likely to disintegrate. Always use new lids to ensure that your canning is successful.

Check for Recent Canning Updates

Canning equipment has changed over the years, becoming more high tech and therefore more efficient at processing foods. In addition to the equipment becoming more advanced, there have also been many scientific improvements, making canning safer when the proper steps are taken. For example, many people used to sterilize their jars before pressure canning. While this is still okay to do, it is not necessary as science has shown that any bacteria in the jars will die when heated to such a high temperature in a pressure canner. Sterilization is an extra step that you just don't need!

Make sure that your food preservation information is all up to date and uses current canning guidelines. Avoid outdated cookbooks and reassess "trusted family methods" to make sure they fit into the most recent criteria for safe canning. When in doubt, check with the US Department of Agriculture's Complete Guide to Home Canning which contains the most recent, up-to-date canning tips.

Pick the Best Ingredients

When choosing a food to can, always get the best food possible. You want to use high quality, perfectly ripe produce for canning. You will never end up with a jar of food better than the produce itself, so picking good ingredients is important to the taste of your final product. Also, produce that is past its prime can affect the ability to can it. If strawberries are over ripe, your jam may come out too runny. If your tomatoes are past their prime, they may not have a high enough pH level to be processed in a water bath. Pick your ingredients well and you will make successful preserved foods.

Clean Everything

While you may know that your jars and lids need to be washed and sanitized, don't forget about the rest of your tools. Cleaning out your canner before using it is essential, even if you put it away clean. Make sure to wipe your countertop well, making sure there are no crumbs or residue. Wash your produce with clean, cold water and don't forget to wash your hands! The cleaner everything is, the less likely you are to spread bacteria onto your jarred foods

Follow Your Recipe

Use recipes from trusted sources and be sure to follow them to the letter. Changing the amount of one or two ingredients may alter the balance of acidity and could result in unsafe canning (especially when using a water bath canner). Use the ingredients as directed and make very few changes—none if possible.

Adhere to the processing times specified by your recipe. Sometimes the times may seem a little long, but the long processing time is what makes these products safe to store on the shelf. The processing time is the correct amount of time needed to destroy spoilage organisms, mold spores, yeast and pathogens in the jar. So, as you may have guessed, it is extremely important to use the times that are written in your recipe as a hard rule.

Cool the Jars

Be sure that you give your jars 12 hours to cool before testing the seal. If you test the seal too early, it may break as the jar is still warm, making the rubber pliable. Be sure to cool the jars away from a window or fan as even a slight breeze may cause the hot jars to crack. Once cool, remove the metal band, clean it and save it for your next canning project.

Don't Risk It

If you suspect that a food you have canned is bad, don't try to eat it, just toss it! Each time you open a jar of canned food, inspect it and check for the following:

- Is the lid bulging, swollen or leaking at all?
- If the jar cracked or damaged?
- Does the jar foam when opened?
- Is the food inside discolored or moldy?

- Does the food smell bad?

If you notice any of these warning signs in a food that you have canned, throw it away. Do not taste it to check if it is good. It is not worth risking your health to try the food after seeing one of the above signs.

Luckily, it is fairly easy to spot a jar of food that has gone bad. Home canned food can spoil for many reasons. A dent in the lid, a small crack in the jar, an improper seal, or not enough processing time are all common errors that may cause canned foods to go bad. Follow the exact canning directions and hopefully you will never get a bad jar of food!

How to Prepare Healthy Canned Foods

Commercially canned foods contain more salt and sugar and this is the reason why home canning is preferred by many because they have control over the amount of sugar and salt that they put in their food. There are many conventional canning recipes that you can make but this book will discuss about healthy canned foods that you can prepare. This is especially true if you live with someone who is required to eat foods less in sugar and salt.

Canning without Using Sugar

Conventional canning methods require the use of sugar to preserve food for a long time. But didn't you know that you can still can and preserve food without using sugar? In canning fruits without sugar, it is important to select fruits that are firm but fully ripe. Avoid choosing fruits that show signs of diseases. Prepare the fruits for hot packs and use unsweetened fruit juices or just regular water to add sweetness to the fruit. However, if you like your preserved fruits sweet, you can always use sugar substitute Splenda© before you process the food for canning.

Canning with Less Salt

Salt serves as a preservative for most foods including meats. If you don't want to use a lot of salt when canning your food because of diet restrictions, then you can still do so without fearing that your food will spoil. The thing is that salt used to can vegetables and meats are used primarily to enhance the flavor and not act as a preservative.

Canning Baby Foods

Baby foods can also be canned so that you can have a stash of prepared meals for your baby each day.

Where To Store

All have tried canned food at least once in a lifetime. Meat, fish, cereals, vegetables, and drinks in cans are so firmly enshrined in a single person's life that it's hard to imagine what we'd do without them now. Canning has repeatedly saved people from hunger, and now saves housewives time to cook dinner.

And while nutritionists are categorically opposed to the use of canned foods, they are considered to be unnatural products and contain harmful food additives, stabilizers and flavor enhancers, yet many cannot refuse them. When buying canned goods, it is necessary to know how to store them so as not to become a victim of a spoiled product.

How to store canned food

You should pay attention to their quality when choosing canned food for consumption in the near future, or for long-term storage. Poor quality canned food may contain botulism toxin, which can lead to severe gastrointestinal tract disease, and the storage of such canned food will exacerbate their condition further. Therefore it is important not only to know how to store and how much canned food but also to choose them correctly.

So, first, you should pay attention to the can when buying canned food-if it has at least the slightest signs of bloating, then it's definitely not recommended to take it.

Second, canned goods with evident signs of damage should not be among the purchases, as dents and chips are one of the causes of depressurization and, consequently, bacterial growth. And finally, like any product, canned food has an expiry date, which is around two years in most cases. If you are planning to buy canned food for long-term storage, then it is safer, of course, to choose the new.

As a rule, canned food is released into a container that is lined with plastic, the inner side of which is varnished, enameled, or half-finished. Thanks to sterilization, which takes place during canned food manufacture and allows them to be stored for more than a year. Boxes or boxes that are in a dry and cool room are the best places to store canned goods.

If canned food is smeared with industrial petroleum jelly in containers, it is best not to extract it until the moment of release, because it will be stored best. The processing of canned food cans is particularly important when they are stored in underground and cellars where a high level of humidity can cause metal corrosion and, as a result, depressurization of containers and damage to the product.

How much to store canned food

If possible, it is necessary to store canned foods so that the cans do not touch each other, so any mechanical damage will cause corrosion. It is worth noting that when talking about canned food shelf-life, manufacturers mean the period of time during which a hole can be formed in a tin due to corrosion.

How long to store open canned food

Eating all the open canned foods isn't always possible; not everyone knows how to store them. If you had to leave a product like this, it's best to transfer it to a plastic or glass container, close it tightly and send it to the fridge. How be much-canned foods stored in open condition? No matter how correctly they do it, the canned food can't be kept for more than three to four days. This is particularly true of canned meat and fish, which it is advisable to use if not immediately after opening, then a maximum of two days.

Chapter 5 : Recipes

Stewed Tomatoes

Ingredients:

- 3 pounds fresh tomatoes
- 1 cup chopped onion
- 3 cloves garlic, minced
- 1 tablespoon dried oregano
- 1 tablespoon olive oil
- 1 teaspoon sugar

Directions:

1. Heat the olive oil in a large pot and add the garlic and onion, cooking and stirring for 10 minutes.

2. Add tomatoes, sugar, and oregano and simmer on low heat for 30–45 minutes, until the tomatoes begin softening and breaking down.

3. Spoon the tomatoes into hot glass jars and wipe the rim to remove any food debris.

4. Screw on the tops and the rings and place in a boiling water bath for 20 minutes.
5. Remove the jars and allow to cool.

Corn - Whole Kernel

Ingredients:

- 20 pounds corn, cut from cob
- 9 teaspoons salt
- 10 cups water

Directions

1. In a large pan, add the water, salt, and corn and bring to a boil. Let it boil for 5 minutes.

2. Fill sterilized jars with the corn and the liquid, leaving a 1 inch of head space. Adjust the jar lids and process the jars in a pressure canner for 55 minutes at 10 pounds of pressure for a pressure canner with a weighted gauge or 11 pounds if the pressure canner has a dial gauge.

White Potatoes - Cubed or Whole

Ingredients:

- 13 pounds potatoes
- 4 tablespoons salt
- Boiling water

Directions

1. Wash and peel the potatoes and place them in acid solution, made up of 1 gallon of water with 1 cup of lemon juice to prevent them from darkening. If you do not want whole potatoes, cut into ½ inch cubes. Drain and cook 2 minutes in boiling salt water, and drain again.

2. For whole potatoes, boil in salt water for 10 minutes and drain. Fill sterilized jars with the potatoes. Cover the potatoes with fresh boiling water, leaving a 1 inch headspace.

3. Process in a pressure canner for 35 minutes at 10 pounds of pressure for a pressure canner with a weighted gauge or 11 pounds if the pressure canner has a dial gauge.

Pickled Beets

Ingredients:

- 6 cups vinegar
- 2 cups water
- 4 cups sugar
- 1 tablespoon ground cinnamon
- ¾ tablespoon salt
- ½ tablespoon ground cloves
- 6 pounds beets, peeled and sliced

Directions:

1. In a heavy stockpot, combine the sugar, white vinegar, cinnamon, water, cloves, and salt. Bring to a boil, and stir until the sugar has dissolved completely.

2. Pack the beets into sterilized jars and cover with the pickling solution, leaving ¼ inch of space at the top.

3. Wipe rims, affix lids and bands, and process in a boiling water bath for 30 minutes.

4. Allow to cool. Refrigerate after opening

Marinated Fava Beans

Ingredients:

- ½ lbs. of fava beans
- **2** tablespoons of red wine vinegar or cooking sherry
- ¼ teaspoon of black ground pepper

- ½ teaspoon of kosher salt
- 2 sprigs of fresh rosemary
- 1 teaspoon garlic, freshly minced
- 2 tablespoons olive oil

Directions:

1. Bring a pot of salted water to a boil. While water is heating up, remove beans from their pods.

2. Once water is boiling add beans, and cook for about 3 minutes or until tender and green.

3. Drain the beans and rinse them under cold water.

4. Pop the fava beans out of their casings and set them aside. In a mason jar mix the olive oil, vinegar, garlic, rosemary sprigs, salt and pepper.

5. Place lid on jar and shake contents to combine. Add fava beans to jar and secure lid. These marinated beans will keep up to three days in the fridge. Allow the beans to soak for at least 15 minutes in the mix before serving them.

6.
Tomatoes - Whole

Ingredients:

- 21 pounds whole tomatoes, skinned
- 4 tablespoons salt
- ¾ cup lemon juice, optional
- Boiling water

Directions

1. Place the tomatoes and the salt in a saucepan and cover with the water. Bring to a boil and cook for 5 minutes.

2. Pack sterilized jars with the tomatoes and the hot liquid, leaving a ½ inch head space. Remove any air bubbles, clean the rim and adjust lids.

3. If omitting the lemon juice, process the jars for 45 minutes in a pressure canner at 10 pounds of pressure for a pressure canner with a weighted gauge or 11 pounds if the pressure canner has a dial gauge.

4. If using lemon juice, process the jars for 10 minutes in a boiling water bath.

Spiced Beets

Ingredients:

- ¼ teaspoon salt
- ¾ teaspoon allspice
- ¾ teaspoon cloves
- ¼ stick cinnamon
- ¼ piece mace
- 1 ½ teaspoons celery seed
- 2 cups cider vinegar, 5% acidity
- 1 cup sugar
- 2 pints beets

Directions

1. Tie the salt and the spices in a thin cloth bag. Boil the vinegar, sugar, and spices for 15 minutes. Sterilize a quart jar for 15 minutes. Remove the jar from the water and pour in the vinegar mixture. Adjust the lid and set aside for 2 weeks.

2. Remove the spice bag. Cook fresh beets until tender but firm, and let cool. Peel the beets. Heat the vinegar and add ½ cup of the beet liquid. Add the beets and simmer for 15 minutes.

3. Pack into sterile jars, being sure the vinegar covers the beets. Remove air bubbles and adjust the lids. Process for 10 minutes in a boiling water bath.

Spicy Green Beans

Ingredients:

- ¼ teaspoon salt
- ¾ teaspoon allspice
- ¾ teaspoon cloves
- ¼ stick cinnamon
- ¼ piece mace
- 1 ½ teaspoons celery seed
- 2 cups cider vinegar, 5% acidity
- 1 cup sugar
- 2 pints green beans

Directions

1. Tie the salt and the spices in thin cloth bag. Boil the vinegar, sugar, and spices for 15 minutes. Sterilize a quart jar for 15 minutes. Remove the jar from the water and pour in the vinegar mixture. Adjust the lid and set aside for 2 weeks.
2. Remove the spice bag. Cook fresh beans until tender but firm, and let cool. Heat the vinegar and add ½ cup of the bean liquid. Add the beans and simmer for 15 minutes.

3. Pack into sterile jars, being sure the vinegar covers the beans. Remove any air bubbles and adjust the jar lids. Process the jars for 10 minutes in a boiling water bath.

Damson Jellies

Ingredients:

- Preserving sugar
- Damsons: 1.8kg
- Lemon Juice: 2 lemons

Directions:

1. Carefully wash the fruits and put into preserving pan along with lemon juice and 300ml water. Let them boil and simmer for almost 30 to 40 minutes, until the fruit turns soft.

2. You have to pour the content of this pan on a scalded bag of jelly with one large set of bowl underneath to catch fallen juices. Leave it for several hours.

3. Now, measure the juice in your pan again and add an equal quantity of sugar, such as 400g sugar to each 400ml juice or 1lb sugar in each pint of this juice. Mix it on a low heat until sugar completely dissolved and increase the heat. Frequently boil until your jelly is set. Test jelly by spooning a little amount on a chilled saucer and let it cool. Push with one finger and if it gets wrinkles, the jelly is ready. If not, make sure to return to the stove again and boil for 5 extra minutes and test in a similar way again. Jelly is ready to eat.

4. If you want to preserve for one year, pour into sterilized jars and let them cool before sealing.

Grape Jelly

Ingredients:

- Red grapes (with seeds): 1kg
- Jam Sugar with pectin: 450g
- Lemon Juice: Squeeze 1 lemon

Directions:

1. Wash grapes and put into a large saucepan and cook on low heat. Cover the saucepan and leave for 5 minutes until you notice juices. Use one potato masher or fork to mash grapes and leave for 10 minutes. Mash them well until the grapes are completely mashed up. Put one kitchen cloth or tea towel in a sieve and set it on the bowl. Pour the mixture of grape on this

cloth and leave this mixture for one hour or one night to let this mixture drip.

2. Now, measure the juice in your pan again and add an equal quantity of sugar, such as 400g sugar to each 400ml juice or 1lb sugar in each pint of this juice. Pour this measured juice and sugar in a saucepan along with lemon juice. Set the pan on a stove on high heat and let them boil. You can skim any scum while boiling and let the mixture bubble until the temperature on the sugar thermometer reaches 105C. In the absence of a thermometer, you can put one small plate in your freezer for almost 5 minutes. Pour a small quantity of this juice on this cold plate. Run your finger on jelly after 1 minute and if you notice slight wrinkles on the jelly, your jelly is ready to eat.

3. If you want to preserve jelly for one year, pour into sterilized jars and let them cool before sealing.

Guava Jelly

Ingredients:

- Guavas: 4 lb.
- Water: 5 1/2 cups
- Vanilla beans (lengthways split): 2
- Cheesecloth
- Sugar: 4 cups
- Lemon juice: 1 tablespoon
- Lime juice: 1 tablespoon

Directions:

1. Carefully remove ends of guavas and cut them lengthways and crossways into

quarters and make thin slices. Add slices of guava in a stainless steel Dutch oven (4-qt) along with water and let them boil. Cover pot and simmer on low heat for 20 minutes. Mix it occasionally.

2. Line 3 dampened cheesecloth in a fine strainer (wire mesh) and put this strainer in a bowl. Pour mixture of guava into the strainer. There is no need to press, just cover the mixture and leave it for a few hours or one night, until you collect the whole juice and dripping stops. The juice will be 4 ½ cups.

3. Carefully scrape seeds of vanilla beans and mix those vanilla beans, vanilla bean seeds, sugar, citrus juice and guava juice in the similar oven. Let this mixture boil on medium heat and mix sugar to dissolve. Reduce flame to medium and simmer for 25 – 30minutes or until you notice gelling point. Turn off heat and discard vanilla beans. You can skim foam, if you find it necessary.

4. Put the jars in simmering water canner. Replicate this process with all jars. Process

jars for almost 10 minutes and adjust their altitude. Turn off heat, remove lids and leave these jars for five minutes. Take out all jars, leave for 24 hours without moving them. Check their vacuum seal and secure for one year.

Strawberry Jellies

Ingredients:

- Fresh strawberries (hulled): 2 pounds
- Lemon juice: ¼ cup
- White sugar: 4 cups

Directions:

1. Take a wide bowl to crush strawberries in small batches to get 4 cups of pounded berries. In one heavy saucepan, mix lemon

juice, strawberries, and sugar. Mix well on low heat until the sugar is dissolved. Now, increase heat to high and let this mixture boil. Mix frequently until the temperate increases to 220 degrees F.

2. Transfer this jam to sterile jars and leave ¼ - ½ inches headspace and seal as per instructions that are given in canning procedure. Process in a water bath and secure for one year.

3.

Apple Jelly

Ingredients:

- Apples (diced and cored): 3 ½ pounds

- Butter: ½ teaspoon
- Water: 3 cups
- Powdered fruit (pectin): 2 ounces
- White sugar: 7 ½ cups

Directions:

1. Put apples in one large pot, cover it with water and let it boil. Reduce heat and cover to simmer until the apples turn tender. It will take almost 5 minutes. Crush all cooked apples and simmer for extra five minutes.

2. Line a sieve with cheesecloth and pour mixture of crushed apples on this sieve. Let this mixture drip for a few hours or whole night. Measure 5 cups juice of apple (you can add water if the juice is less than 5 cups) and stir sugar in this juice. Add butter to decrease foaming.

3. Put this mixture in pot again and let it boil. Mix constantly and stir pectin in this mixture as well. Boil for almost 1 minute to completely dissolve pectin and mix

constantly. Turn off heat and discard extra foam with metal spoon.

4. In order to can this jelly, you have to follow canning procedure given in the beginning.

Corn Cob Jelly

Ingredients:

- Corn: 12 ears
- Water: 4 cups
- Fruit pectin: 1 box powdered
- Sugar: 4 cups
- Food color: Yellow

Directions:

1. Cut kernels of corn from cobs and secure these kernels to use in any other recipe.

2. Take one large pot and put cobs and water in this pot. Bring them to boiling point and let them boil for almost 10 minutes.

3. Strain this liquid through cheesecloth and discard cobs. The liquid should be three cups or you can add additional water as per your needs. You have to bring it to a rolling boil and add sugar. Bring it to boil again and boil for almost one minute.

4. Turn off heat and remove foam from the top. You can add a few drops of yellow food color and pour in hot mason jars. You have to follow canning instructions to seal these jars.

Jalapeno Jelly

Ingredients:

- Bell pepper (Green): 1
- Jalapeno peppers: 12
- Apple vinegar: 1 ½ cups
- Granulated sugar: 4 ¼ cups
- Liquid pectin: 4 ounces
- Jalapeno peppers (remove seeds and finely chopped): 4
- Salt: 1 pinch

Directions:

1. Take a food processor or blender to blend jalapeno peppers (12) and bell pepper in this processor (you can do in small batches

as well). You have to make them finely chopped.

2. Transfer these peppers in one saucepan and mix vinegar and let them boil. These should simmer for 15 – 20 minutes. Use two layers of cheesecloth and strain mixture through them and throw pulp. This liquid should be 1 cup.

3. Return this liquid to saucepan and mix sugar and salt to dissolve them completely. Let them boil on medium heat and once the mixture starts to rolling boil (that can't be stirred down), boil for almost 1 minute. Mix liquid pectin in this mixture and mix leftover jalapeno peppers. Pour in mason jar and leave ¼ inch space from top. To secure this jelly for one year, make sure to follow canning process.

Dandelion Jelly

Ingredients:

- Water: 4 cups

- Dandelion blossoms (white and yellow parts only): 4 cups

- Powdered pectin: ¼ cup + 1 ½ teaspoons

- Granulated sugar: 4 ½ cups

- Lemon juice: 2 tablespoons

Directions:

1. Take a pot and put dandelion blossoms and water in this pot. Let them boil and decrease heat to medium. The liquid should simmer for almost 3 minutes. Turn off heat and leave it for 10 minutes.

2. Use one fine sieve to strain this mixture into a measuring cup and press flowers gently to squeeze liquid. Discard blossoms and secure liquid. This liquid should be 3 cups; otherwise, you can add some water to make it 3 cups.

3. Take a bowl and mix pectin and ½ cup sugar. Pour remaining sugar (4 cups) and dandelion liquid in a pan and let them boil. Stir on a constant basis to completely dissolve sugar and add pectin mixture as well. Stir them again to completely dissolve pectin and add the juice of a lemon. Let them boil for one minute and skim foam that may be floating on the surface. Let them cool and follow the canning process to secure in a mason jar.

Orange Jelly

Ingredients:

- Concentrated orange juice: 6 ounces
- Water: 2 ½ cup
- White sugar: 4 ½ cup
- Canning jars with rings and lids: 6 (half pint)
- Powdered pectin (fruit): 1.75 ounce

Directions:

1. Put orange juice, pectin and water in a saucepan. Let them boil on high heat and mix constantly. Once you notice boiling

point, add sugar and reduce heat to return this mixture to simmer. Stir constantly.

2. Boil for one minute and turn off heat. Discard any foam floated on the top of this mixture. Your jelly is ready; you can secure it for one year with the help of canning procedure given on the top.

Garlic Jelly

Ingredients:

- Peeled Garlic Cloves: ¼ cup
- White vinegar: 2 cups
- White sugar: 5 cups
- Liquid pectin: 3 ounces

Directions:

1. Take a blender or food processor to blend garlic and vinegar (1/2 cup) to make a smooth mixture.

2. Put this mixture in a saucepan along with sugar and leftover vinegar. Keep it on high heat and let this mixture boil. Stir on a constant basis and quickly add pectin.

3. Let this mixture boil hard once again for one minute. Mix constantly and turn off heat. Jelly is ready.

4. You have to follow the canning procedure to secure this jelly for one year.

Mint Jelly

Ingredients:

- Fresh Mint stem and leaves: 1 ½ cups
- Food color (green): 1 drop
- Lemon Juice: 2 tablespoons
- White sugar: 3 ½ cups
- Boiling water: 2 ¼ cups
- Liquid pectin: ½ container or 6 ounce

Directions:

1. Carefully wash mint leaves and put them in a large saucepan. You can crush them with the bottom of one glass. Now, add water

and let the mint boil. Turn off heat and cover for almost 10 minutes. Strain this liquid and measure 1 2/3 cups of liquid.

2. Put this liquid in one saucepan and mix food color and lemon juice. It is time to mix sugar and put this pan on high heat. Let them boil and stir on a constant basis. Add pectin and mix again. Boil this mixture for one minute to full and stir constantly.

3. Turn off heat and skim the foam floating on the top with the help of one metal spoon. Transfer this blend in sterile jars and seal by following canning process.

Cherry Jelly

Ingredients:

- Cherry juice: 3 ½ cups
- Water: 1 cup
- Dry pectin: 1 ¾ ounce
- Sugar: 4 ½ cups

Directions:

1. To make juice, get ripe cherries and wash them softly. Remove their stems and put in a large pot. Use a potato masher to crush cherries. Put these mashed cherries in a saucepan and add one cup water in this pan. Let them boil and decrease heat to simmer for ten minutes. Strain juice

through one cheesecloth or fine mesh. Mix peels, pits and pulp.

Jelly Directions:

1. Take 3 ½ cups juice in a large cooking pot and add pectin. Mix it well and increase heat to high. Let them fully boil and add sugar in this mixture. Stir constantly and let this mixture fully boil again. Turn off heat and discard foam from top. Jelly is ready, pour this mixture in sterilized bottled and follow canning procedure to seal their lids.

Mango Jelly

Ingredients

- Hard and ripe mango slices: ½ kg

- Sugar: 3 cups

- Water: 1 ¾ cups

- Lemon juice: 1 lemon

Directions:

1. Take a deep pan and put mango slices in this pan along with water. Cook until tender. Turn off heat and mash mango slices with a potato masher. Turn off heat and pass it through a cheesecloth or gravy strainer.

2. Put this juice in the pot again and put sugar, mango pulp and juice of a lemon. Cook on high heat and mix constantly, until jelly completely sets. Test this jelly and leave for a few minutes. Pour into sterilized jars and follow canning procedure to secure for one year.

Ginger Jelly

Ingredients:

- Fresh cranberries: 12-ounce
- Sugar: 2 cups
- Peeled and Grated ginger: 2 teaspoons
- Unflavored gelatin: 1 tablespoon

Directions:

1. Take a medium saucepan and add cranberries, ginger, water and sugar in this pan. Let them boil on high heat, reduce heat and let them simmer for almost 10 minutes. Mix occasionally and let them soft. Pass this mixture through one sieve into a bowl by pressing pulp with a wooden spoon. Try to extract as much liquid as you can and discard pulps.

2. In the meantime, sprinkle gelatin in a bowl with ½ cup water and leave for 5 minutes. Add cranberry mixture to this bowl and mix gelatin to completely dissolve. Pour in an airtight jar and follow canning procedure to secure it. If you don't want to can, you can pour in a mason jar and freeze simply in the freezer.

3.

Hot Jelly

Ingredients:

- Red pepper (hot): 2 cups minced

- Red wine: 1 cup

- Habanero pepper (minced): 2 cups

- Pomegranate juice: ½ cup

- Lemon juice: 1 tablespoon
- Powdered pectin (fruit): 1.75 ounce
- Butter: 1 teaspoon
- White sugar: 4 cups
- Red wine: 1 cup

Directions:

1. Blend wine and red pepper in one blender, but make sure to wear gloves before touching peppers. Blend them to make a smooth paste and transfer this mixture to one large pot.

2. Blend pomegranate juice, lemon juice, and habanero pepper in a blender to get a smooth paste. Add it in a pot and mix butter and pectin as well. Mix them well and bring this mixture to fully boil and mix sugar.

3. Constantly mix sugar to dissolve for almost 2 minutes. Turn off heat and stir for almost five minutes. Remove foam floating on the top of mixture. Jelly is ready. You have to

follow canning procedure to preserve this jelly.

Mango Jams

Ingredients:

- Water: ¾ cup
- Ripe mangoes: 2 pounds
- White sugar: 1 ½ cups
- Saffron threads: 3 (optional)

Directions:

1. Boil whole mangoes to make them soft and leave for a few minutes to let them cool. Remove peels and inner seeds of mango to

get the pulp. Put this pulp in a bowl and mash with a fork or masher. Keep it aside.

2. Take a saucepan and put sugar and water in it to cook on low heat. Stir them well to dissolve sugar and increase heat to medium to let them boil. Once you notice soft thread and 270 degrees F temperature on a sugar thermometer, you can mix mango pulp and saffron. Mix them well and cook for almost 5 minutes. Pour this jam into your sterilized jars and seal these jars as per canning instructions.

Strawberry Jam

Ingredients:

- Fresh strawberries (hulled): 3 pounds
- Lemon juice: ¼ cup
- White sugar: 4 ½ cups

Directions:

1. Take a wide bowl to crush strawberries in small batches to get 6 cups of pounded berries. In one heavy saucepan, mix lemon juice, strawberries, and sugar. Mix well on low heat until the sugar is dissolved. Now, increase heat to high and let this mixture boil. Mix frequently until the temperate increases to 220 degrees F.

2. Transfer this jam to sterile jars .

Peach Jam

Ingredients:

- Fresh strawberries (hulled): 3 pounds
- Lemon juice: ¼ cup
- White sugar: 4 ½ cups

Directions:

1. Take a wide bowl to crush strawberries in small batches to get 6 cups of pounded berries. In one heavy saucepan, mix lemon juice, strawberries, and sugar. Mix well on low heat until the sugar is dissolved. Now, increase heat to high and let this mixture

boil. Mix frequently until the temperate increases to 220 degrees F.

2. Transfer this jam to sterile jars and leave ¼ - ½ inches headspace and seal as per instructions that are given in canning procedure. Process in a water bath and secure for one year.

Blueberry Jam

Ingredients:

- Fresh blueberries: 8 cups
- Lemon juice: ¼ cup
- White sugar: 6 cups

- Ground cinnamon: 2 teaspoons
- Lemon peel (grated): 2 teaspoons
- Nutmeg (ground): ½ teaspoon
- Liquid pectin (fruit): 6 ounces

Directions:

1. Take a food process and process blueberries in a blender. In one heavy saucepan, mix lemon juice, processed blueberries, cinnamon, nutmeg, lemon peel and sugar. Mix well on low heat until the sugar is dissolved. Now, increase heat to high and let this mixture boil. Add pectin and let them boil for one minute again. Mix frequently to dissolve sugar and pectin. Turn off heat and remove foam on the top of this mixture.

2. Transfer this jam to sterile jars and leave ¼ - ½ inches headspace and seal as per instructions that are given in canning procedure. Process in a water bath and secure for one year.

Peach Jam

Ingredients:

- Chopped Peaches (peeled and pitted): 8 cups
- Lemon juice: 4 tablespoons
- Fruit pectin (powdered): 6 tablespoons
- Sugar: 7 cups
- Finely chopped ginger: 1 tablespoon
- Grated gingerroot: ¼ teaspoon
- Ground nutmeg: ½ teaspoon
- Ground cinnamon: ½ teaspoon
- Ground Cloves: ¼ teaspoon

- Ground Allspice: ¼ teaspoon
- Lemon zest: ½ lemon

Directions:

1. Take a pan and put lemon juice and peaches in this bowl. Let them boil on medium heat and then add pectin to let this mixture boil again. Stir on a constant basis and slowly mix sugar. Add ginger, nutmeg, ginger root, allspice, cinnamon, nutmeg, lemon zest and cloves in this mixture. Continue to boil and mix constantly for almost one minute.

2. Turn off heat and remove any skim foam from the top of this jam. Carefully pour jam in sterilized bottle while leaving ¼ inch headspace empty and follow canning procedure to seal its lid.

Tomato Jam

Ingredients:

- Large lemons: 4
- Pulp tomatoes (cored and 1-inch pieces): 4 /12 pounds
- Ground cumin: 4 teaspoons
- Brown sugar: 4 cups
- Kosher salt as per taste
- Red pepper flakes: 2 teaspoons
- Cinnamon sticks: 4
- Ground cloves: ½ teaspoon
- Peeled ginger: 8 1/8 inch

Directions:

1. Peel lemons and vegetables with a vegetable peeler and leave their bitter pith behind. Put a strainer on cooking pan and squeeze lemon juice on the strainer.

2. Add sugar, cumin, lemon zest, and tomatoes along with 4 teaspoons salt, cinnamon, ginger, cloves, sticks and pepper flakes. Cook them on medium heat and mix occasionally to dissolve sugar and make tomatoes juicy.

3. It will take almost 15 to 20 minutes. Add a candy thermometer to register almost 220 degrees F. It may take 40 – 50 minutes. Reduce flame to avoid scorching of mixture and discard cinnamon sticks.

4. Sterilize mason jars as per canning instructions and fill these jars to seal them professionally.

Orange Jam

Ingredients:

- Concentrated orange juice: 8 ounces
- Water: 3 ½ cup
- White sugar: 5 ½ cup
- Orange peel (grated): 3 tablespoons
- Powdered pectin (fruit): 2 ounce

Directions:

1. Put orange juice, pectin and water in a saucepan. Let them boil on high heat and mix constantly. Once you notice boiling

point, orange peel, add sugar and reduce heat to return this mixture to simmer.

2. Stir constantly. Boil for one minute and turn off heat. Discard any foam floating on the top of this mixture.

3. Your jam is ready; you can secure it for one year with the help of canning procedure given on the top.

Fig Jam

Ingredients:

- Sugar: 3 ½ cups

- Candied ginger: 1 tablespoon

- Fresh blossoms of lavender: 2 tablespoons
- Fresh fig: 1 ¾ lbs
- Lemon zest and juice: 1 lemon
- Pine nuts: 2 tablespoons

Directions:

1. Put sugar, ginger, and lavender in a blender and blend them well. Put this mixture in a pot with a heavy bottom. Now, add lemon juice, zest, and figs in the processor. Pulse for almost 5 to 6 times to chop them coarsely. Add this in the pot with sugar.

2. Heat them on medium heat and let them boil then increase heat for almost 15 minutes and stir frequently During cooking, the juice turns a vibrant red. Add pine nuts and turn off the stove. Pour this mixture into sterilized jars as per the instructions of the canning process.

Cherry Jam with Sour Taste

Ingredients:

- Sour cherries: 3 lbs or 4 cups
- Sugar: 7 cups
- Fruit pectin (liquid): 6 ounces
- Almond extract: 1 teaspoon

Directions:

1. Wash cherries, pit and stem them. Chop them to make their small pieces. Take a saucepan and put fruit and sugar in this pan.

2. Boil them for one minute and turn off heat. It is time to mix liquid pectin in this saucepan and mix for 5 minutes.

3. Add almond extracts and put this jam into sterilized jars according to the canning instructions.

Apple Jam

Ingredients:

- Apples (chopped and tart apples): 4 cups
- Lemon juice: 1 ½ tablespoons
- Cinnamon: 1 teaspoon
- Nutmeg: ¼ teaspoon
- Ginger: ¼ teaspoon
- Sugar: 4 cups
- Brown sugar: 1 cup
- Dry pectin: 1 ¾ ounce

- Butter: 1 teaspoon

Directions:

1. Take a cooking pan and put water after measuring 4 cups and apples. Add butter, spices, lemon juice and pectin in this pan. Let them boil and add sugar. Bring this mixture to fully boil again and simmer for 1 minute. Mix constantly, remove from heat and skim off the foam on the top of this mixture.

2. Pour this mixture into sterilized mason jars leaving ¼" headspace and follow canning instructions to seal the lid.

Almond and Cherry Jam

Ingredients:

- Pitted cherries (chopped): 1 quart
- Dry pectin: 1 packet
- Lemon juice: ¼ cup
- Almond liqueur: ¼ cup
- Almond extract: 1 teaspoon
- Cinnamon: ½ teaspoon
- Ground cloves: ½ teaspoon
- Sugar: 4 ½ cups

Directions:

1. Take a saucepan and combine all ingredients except sugar. Let them boil and mix constantly.

2. Add sugar and stir again constantly to completely dissolve sugar. Boil for two minutes again and mix constantly. Turn off heat and skim floating foam on the surface.

3. Ladle into sterilized jars as per canning instructions.

Jalapeno Jam

Ingredients:

- Strawberries (crushed): 4 cups
- Jalapeno peppers (minced): 1 cup
- Lemon juice: ¼ cup
- Fruit pectin: 2 ounce
- White sugar: 7 cups
- 8 mason jar with lids and rings for canning

Directions:

1. Take a large saucepan and put crushed strawberries, jalapeno pepper, pectin and lemon juice in this pan.

2. Let them boil on high heat and reduce heat to let them simmer to dissolve sugar

completely. After dissolving sugar, return this mixture to boil and simmer for one minute.

3. Jam is ready, pour into sterilized jars according to the canning instructions.

Pear Jam

Ingredients:

- Pear (ripe, cored and mashed): 4 1/2 cups
- Lemon juice: 1 ½ tablespoons
- Cinnamon: 1 teaspoon
- Nutmeg: ¼ teaspoon

- Ground cloves: ½ teaspoon
- Ginger: ¼ teaspoon
- Sugar: 4 cups
- White sugar: 7 1/2 cup
- Fruit pectin: 3 tablespoons
- Butter: 1 teaspoon

Directions:

1. Take a cooking pan and put water after measuring 4 cups and pears. Add butter, cloves, spices, lemon juice and pectin in this pan. Let them boil and add sugar. Bring this mixture to fully boil again and simmer for 1 minute. Mix constantly, remove from heat and skim off the foam on the top of this mixture.

2. Pour this mixture into sterilized mason jars leaving ¼" headspace and follow canning instructions to seal the lid.

Mixed Fruit Jam

Ingredients:

- Mixed fruit: 1 kg (peeled & chopped)
- Sugar: 1 kg
- Lemon juice: ¼ cup or more as per taste

Directions:

1. Take a glass or steel container and put fruits in this container. Fill it with water and keep for the whole night. In the morning, transfer this liquid to a saucepan with a heavy base and let them boil. Cook to tender all fruits and strain through a cheesecloth or soup strainer.

2. Slowly press pulp to squeeze juice completely and put this liquid again on the stove. Let them boil and stir constantly to avoid scorching. Once you get a slightly thinner mixture, add lemon juice and sugar.

3. Reduce heat and stir constantly to dissolve sugar. Once the sugar is dissolved, increase heat and let this mixture boil. Test this jam by dropping one drop over a cold surface and store in sterilized jars as per canning instructions.

Kiwi Jam

Ingredients:

- Peeled and chopped Kiwi: 3 cups

- Dry pectin: 1 package
- Pineapple juice (unsweetened): 1 cup
- Sugar: 4 cups

Directions:

1. Take a saucepan and combine pectin, pineapple juice, and Kiwi. Let them boil, but stir constantly. Add sugar and mix to dissolve sugar.

2. Return this blend to rolling boil for one minute, but mix constantly. Turn off heat and remove any foam on the top of its surface. Jam is ready and you can pour this jam in sterilized jars as per canning instructions.

3.

Double Berry Jelly

Ingredients:

- 3 half-pint jars with bands and lids
- 1 ½ cups fresh raspberries
- 1 ½ cups fresh blackberries
- 2 tablespoons fruit pectin
- 1 ½ cups white sugar

Directions:

1. Prepare your water bath canner as well as your lids and bands according to the step-by-step guide.

2. Combine the raspberries and blackberries in a large saucepan and crush them with a potato masher.

3. Stir in the pectin then bring the mixture to boil while stirring constantly.

4. Add the sugar and stir until dissolved then return to a boil for 1 minute.

5. Remove from heat and skim the foam then spoon the mixture into your jars, leaving about ¼-inch of headspace.

6. Clean the rims, add the lid and seal with a metal band.

7. Place the jars in the water bath canner and bring the water to boil.

8. Process the jars for 10 minutes then remove the jars and wipe them dry.

9. Place the jars on a canning rack and cool for 24 hours before storing.

Blueberry Jam

Ingredients:

- 4 half-pint jars with lids and bands
- 3 tablespoons fruit pectin
- 3 cups fresh blueberries
- 2 tablespoons fresh lemon juice
- ½ teaspoon unsalted butter
- 3 cups white sugar

Directions:

1. Prepare your water bath canner as well as your lids and bands according to the step-by-step guide.

2. Sprinkle the pectin in the bottom of a large saucepan.

3. Add the blueberries and mash them gently with a potato masher.

4. Stir in the lemon juice and butter then bring to a boil.

5. Add the sugar then cook until the sugar is dissolved, stirring constantly.

6. Remove from heat then spoon the mixture into your jars, leaving about ½-inch of headspace.

7. Clean the rims, add the lid and seal with a metal band.

8. Place the jars in the water bath canner and bring the water to boil.

9. Process the jars for 10 minutes then remove the jars and wipe them dry.

10. Place the jars on a canning rack and cool for 24 hours before storing.

Lemon Strawberry Marmalade

Ingredients:

- 6 or 7 half-pint jars with lids and bands
- 4 lbs. fresh strawberries, mashed with a potato masher
- 1 tablespoon fresh lemon juice
- 1/3 cup fruit pectin
- 6 cups white sugar

Directions:

1. Prepare your water bath canner as well as your lids and bands according to the step-by-step guide.

2. Combine the strawberries and lemon juice in a large saucepan.

3. Stir in the pectin then bring the mixture to boil while stirring constantly.

4. Add the sugar and stir until completely dissolved then return to a boil for 1 minute.

5. Remove from heat and skim the foam then spoon the mixture into your jars, leaving about ¼-inch of headspace.

6. Clean the rims, add the lid and seal with a metal band.

7. Place the jars in the water bath canner and bring the water to boil.

8. Process the jars for 10 minutes then remove the jars and wipe them dry.

9. Place the jars on a canning rack and cool for 24 hours before storing.

Salsa Verde

Ingredients:

- 3 glass pint jars with lids and bands
- 12 medium green tomatoes, cored, peeled and diced
- 6 to 8 jalapenos, seeded and minced
- 2 large red onion, diced
- 1 teaspoon minced garlic
- ½ cup fresh lime juice
- ½ cup fresh chopped cilantro
- 1 ½ teaspoons ground cumin
- 1 teaspoon dried oregano

- Salt and pepper to taste

Directions:

1. Prepare your water bath canner as well as your lids and bands.

2. Combine the tomatoes, jalapenos, onion, garlic and lime juice in a large saucepan.

3. Cover and bring to a boil then stir in the remaining ingredients.

4. Reduce heat and simmer for 5 minutes then spoon the mixture into your jars, leaving about ½-inch of headspace.

5. Clean the rims, add the lid and seal with a metal band then place the jars in the water bath canner and bring the water to boil.

6. Process the jars for 20 minutes then remove the jars and wipe them dry.

7. Place the jars on a canning rack and cool for 24 hours before storing.

Spicy Pineapple Salsa

Ingredients:

- 3 glass pint jars with bands and lids
- 4 cups fresh chopped mango
- 2 cups fresh chopped pineapple
- 1 cup seedless golden raisins
- ½ cup diced poblano peppers, seeded
- ¾ cup fresh lemon juice
- ¾ cup fresh lime juice
- ½ cup canned pineapple juice
- 1 green onion, sliced thin
- 2 tablespoons fresh chopped cilantro

- 2 tablespoons brown sugar

Directions:

1. Prepare your water bath canner as well as your lids and bands.

2. Combine all of the ingredients in a large saucepan then cover and bring to boil.

3. Reduce heat and simmer for 5 minutes then spoon into your jars, leaving about ½-inch of headspace.

4. Clean the rims, add the lid and seal with a metal band then place the jars in the water bath canner and bring the water to boil.

5. Process the jars for 15 minutes then remove the jars and wipe them dry.

6. Place the jars on a canning rack and cool for 24 hours before storing.

Zesty Tomato Salsa

Ingredients:

- 4 glass pint jars with lids and bands
- 4 lbs. vine ripened tomatoes, diced
- 1/3 cup distilled white vinegar
- 3 tablespoons crushed red pepper flakes
- 3 tablespoons dried chopped onion
- 1 tablespoon dried cilantro
- 2 teaspoons dried parsley
- 2 teaspoons dried garlic
- 2 teaspoons canning salt
- ½ teaspoon black pepper

Directions:

1. Prepare your water bath canner as well as your lids and bands according to the step-by-step guide.

2. Combine the tomatoes, vinegar and spices in a large saucepan.

3. Cover and bring to a boil then reduce heat and simmer for 5 minutes.

4. Spoon the mixture into your jars, leaving about ½-inch of headspace.

5. Clean the rims, add the lid and seal with a metal band then place the jars in the water bath canner and bring the water to boil.

6. Process the jars for 35 minutes then remove the jars and wipe them dry.

7. Place the jars on a canning rack and cool for 24 hours before storing.

Tropical Fruit Salsa

Ingredients:

- 4 glass half-pint jars with lids and bands
- 6 cups fresh chopped mango
- 1 small red pepper, cored and diced
- ⅓ cup diced sweet onion
- 1 small jalapeno, seeded and minced
- 2 tablespoons fresh lemon juice
- 2 tablespoons white sugar
- ½ cup apple cider vinegar

Directions:

1. Prepare your water bath canner as well as your lids and bands according to the step-by-step guide.

2. Combine the ingredients a large saucepan.

3. Cover and bring to a boil then reduce heat and simmer for 5 minutes.

4. Spoon the mixture into your jars, leaving about ½-inch of headspace.

5. Clean the rims, add the lid and seal with a metal band then place the jars in the water bath canner and bring the water to boil.

6. Process the jars for 20 minutes then remove the jars and wipe them dry.

7. Place the jars on a canning rack and cool for 24 hours before storing.

Sweet Plum Chutney

Ingredients:

- 2 ½ lbs. fresh plums
- ½ cup white sugar
- ½ cup apple cider vinegar
- 4 whole star anise

Directions:

1. Prepare your water bath canner as well as your lids and bands according to the step-by-step guide.

2. Remove the pits from the plums and chop them into 1-inch pieces.

3. Combine the sugar, vinegar and star anise in a saucepan and bring to boil.

4. Stir in the plums then reduce heat and simmer for 5 minutes.

5. Remove from heat and cool for 5 minutes then spoon the mixture into your jars, leaving about ½-inch of headspace.

6. Clean the rims, add the lid and seal with a metal band.

7. Place the jars in the water bath canner and bring the water to boil.

8. Process the jars for 10 minutes then remove the jars and wipe them dry with a clean cloth.

9. Place the jars on a canning rack and cool for 24 hours before storing.

Apricot Pear Chutney

Ingredients:

- 3 cups fresh pears, peeled, cored and diced
- 1 ½ cups dried apricots, chopped
- 2/3 cup brown sugar, packed
- 2/3 cup apple cider vinegar
- ½ cup seedless golden raisins
- ¼ cup crystalized ginger, chopped
- ½ teaspoon ground coriander
- Salt and pepper to taste

Directions:

1. Prepare your water bath canner as well as your lids and bands according to the step-by-step guide.

2. Combine all of the ingredients in a large saucepan.

3. Bring the mixture to boil then reduce heat and simmer for 25 minutes until thick.

4. Spoon the mixture into your jars, leaving about ½-inch of headspace.

5. Clean the rims, add the lid and seal with a metal band.

6. Place the jars in the water bath canner and bring the water to boil.

7. Process the jars for 10 minutes then remove the jars and wipe them dry.

8. Place the jars on a canning rack and cool for 24 hours before storing.

Lime Jelly

Ingredients

- Two cups of unsweetened apple juice
- Three and a half cups of sugar
- One pouch of pectin (liquid)
- One bottle of key lime flavoring

Directions:

1. In a large pot, with a heavy bottom, add the apple juice and mix in the sugar. Turn on the heat and bring the mixture to a full boil – a boil that cannot be stirred down.

2. Stir in the pectin and allow the mixture to boil for one minute.

3. Stir in the key lime flavoring

4. Use a spoon to skim off any unwanted foam

5. Remove jars from the simmering pot and use a ladle, or a similar utensil, to scoop the jelly into the jars. Leave a quarter of an inch of headspace.

6. Seal the jars and place them in the water bath canner. Processing time for this mixture is *ten minutes*.

7. Remove the jars from the canner and allow them to cool down for twenty four hours. Check the lids for sealing and place the sealed jars in a cool, dry storage space.

Pickled Peaches

Ingredients:

- 3 pounds of peaches that have been peeled, pitted and cut in halves
- Three cups of sugar
- One and three-quarter cups of white vinegar
- A cinnamon stick (2 inches)
- One teaspoon of whole cloves
- One teaspoon of juniper berries

Preparation process:

This recipe is designed for two pint jars. If you would like to make more, adjust the measurements accordingly. (If you want to make double the batch, double the measurements in the recipe)

Ensure that your jars are sterilized and being kept heated in a simmering pot

Directions:

1. Combine the sugar and the vinegar in a large stainless steel pot. Bring the mixture to a boil; stir the sugar in until it dissolves completely.

2. Combine the cinnamon, clove and juniper berries in a spice bag or a spice ball. Add the spice ball and peaches to the mixture in the stainless steel pot.

3. Allow the mixture to simmer for ten minutes – or until the peaches are cooked. Make sure that the peaches aren't too soft. Stir the peaches tenderly to ensure that they cook on all sides.

4. Cover the pot and let it stand in a cool area – not the fridge – for three hours. Stir the

peaches a couple of times during this period.

5. Return the pot to the stove and heat the peaches, bringing them to a boil, for two minutes.

6. Remove the pot from the heat and remove the spice ball form the pot.

7. Remove the jars from the simmering pot and place them on a towel. Use a canning funnel to pour the peaches into your jars. Leave one and a half inches of headspace.

8. Use a damp cloth to clean the rims of the jars. Seal the lids and apply the bands, adjusting them until they are as tight as possible.

9. Place your jars in the canning rack and make sure the jars are covered by one to two inches. Cover the canner with its lid.

10. Processing time for this recipe is *twenty minutes.*

11. Remove the jars from the pot and place them on a towel. Allow the jars to cool overnight.

12. Test the lids for sealing and store the sealed jars in a cool, dry storage space.

Tomato Salsa

Ingredients:

- Seven cups of tomatoes – peeled and chopped.

- Two cups of long green chilies – seeded and chopped

- Two and a half cups of chopped onion

- A quarter of a cup of jalapeno peppers – finely chopped and seeded

- Three cloves of finely chopped garlic

- One cup of bottled lemon juice

- One tablespoon of salt

- Half a tablespoon of black pepper

- A quarter of a cup of (fresh) cilantro

- One tablespoon of Greek oregano

Note: You do not need to peel the jalapeno peppers or the green chilies.

Directions:

1. Combine all of the ingredients – except for the oregano and the cilantro – in a cast iron pot.

2. Turn on the heat and stir the mixture frequently until it comes to a boil.

3. Reduce the heat and allow the mixture to simmer for ten minutes. Stir occasionally.

4. Add the oregano and the cilantro to the mixture and allow it to simmer for another twenty minutes. Stir occasionally.

5. Use a ladle to scoop the salsa into the jars. Leave half an inch of headspace.

6. Use a knife to remove any air bubbles and clean the rims of the jars with a clean, damp cloth.

7. Apply the lids and bands, and place the jars in the canner.

8. Processing time for this recipe is *fifteen minutes.*

9. Remove the jars from the canner and place them on a towel. Allow them to cool for

twenty-four hours. Check the lids for sealing and store the sealed jars in a cool, dry storage space.

NB: The only safe changes that you can make to this recipe are the amount of spices and herbs that you add. *Do not* change the proportions of vegetables to acid and tomatoes – this will increase the risk of the salsa becoming contaminated. Do not use vinegar instead of lemon juice.

If you would like to change the pepper, you can use serrano peppers or habaneros instead of jalapenos. Do not add anything else.

Fig Jam

Ingredients

- 3 pounds fresh figs, stemmed and cut into eighths
- 1 cup sugar, divided
- ¾ cup honey
- ½ cup brandy
- Peel of 1 lemon
- Juice of 1 lemon
- 1 teaspoon kosher salt
- 3 tablespoons light pectin

Directions:

1. In a preserving pot or deep saucepot, combine the figs, ¾ cup of sugar, the honey, brandy, lemon peel, lemon juice, and kosher salt. Set aside for 1 hour so the sugar can start to draw out the fig juices and dissolve.

2. Prepare a hot water bath. Place the jars in it to keep warm. Wash the lids and rings in hot, soapy water, and set aside.

3. Remove the lemon peel from the pot and place the pot over medium heat. Bring to a simmer, stirring frequently. Reduce the heat to low. Simmer for about 1 hour, stirring frequently, or until the jam is thick and reduced.

4. With a handheld blender or potato masher, purée the figs. Return the mixture to a simmer.

5. Whisk together the pectin and the remaining ¼ cup of sugar. Whisk this into the jam until there are no lumps. Boil the jam for 1 minute more.

6. Ladle the jam into the prepared jars, leaving ¼ inch of headspace. Use a nonmetallic utensil to release any air bubbles. Wipe the rims clean and seal with the lids and rings.

7. Process the jars in a hot water bath for 10 minutes. Turn off the heat and let the jars rest in the water bath for 10 minutes.

8. Carefully remove the jars from the hot water canner. Set aside to cool for 12 hours.

9. Check the lids for proper seals. Remove the rings, wipe the jars, label and date them, and transfer to a cupboard or pantry.

10. Refrigerate any jars that don't seal properly, and use within 6 weeks. Properly sealed jars will last in the cupboard for 12 months. Once opened, refrigerate and consume within 6 weeks.

Ginger Nectarine Jam

Ingredients
- ½ pounds nectarines, pitted, peeled, and chopped
- 1½ cups sugar
- 2 tablespoons freshly squeezed lemon juice
- 2 tablespoons minced candied ginger
- 1 tablespoon finely grated fresh ginger
- 2 teaspoons ground ginger

Directions:
1. Prepare a hot water bath. Place the jars in it to keep warm. Wash the lids and rings in hot, soapy water, and set aside.
2. In a preserving pot set over low heat, combine the nectarines, sugar, lemon juice, candied ginger, fresh ginger, and ground ginger. Bring to a simmer. Cook for 40 to 45 minutes, stirring often, or until the jam gels and the mixture reaches 220°F, measured with a candy thermometer. Test for gel after 40 minutes.
3. Ladle the jam into the headspace to about ¼ inch of the way. Release any present air bubbles using a nonmetallic utensil. Clean the rims and seal with the lids and rings.
4. Process the jars in a hot water bath for 10 minutes. Turn off the heat and let the jars rest in the water bath for 10 minutes.
5. Carefully remove the jars from the hot water canner. Set aside to cool for 12 hours.
6. Check the lids for proper seals. Remove the rings, wipe the jars, label

and date them, and transfer to a cupboard or pantry.
7. Refrigerate any jars that don't seal properly, and use within 1 month. Properly sealed jars will last in the cupboard for 12 months. Once opened, refrigerate and consume within 1 month.

Blackberry & Apple Jam

Ingredients

- 2 large cooking apples, cored and thinly sliced, cores reserved

- 3 pounds fresh blackberries

- 5 cups sugar

- 3 tablespoons freshly squeezed lemon juice

- 2 to 3 tablespoons blackberry or raspberry cordial, or liqueur (optional)

Directions:

1. Prepare a hot water bath. Place the jars in it to keep warm. Wash the lids and rings in hot, soapy water, and set aside.

2. Put the reserved apple cores in a piece of cheesecloth and tie the ends securely with kitchen twine into a sachet.

3. In a preserving pot or deep pot, combine the apple slices, blackberries, and the sachet. Cover the fruit with water. Bring to a simmer over medium heat and cook for about 10 minutes, stirring frequently, or until the fruit is very tender and starting to fall apart.

4. Remove the pot from the heat. Remove and discard the sachet.

5. Using a sieve or fine strainer, purée the fruit by passing it through into a clean pan.

6. Add the sugar, lemon juice, and cordial (if using). Return the mixture to a simmer over low heat.

7. Continue to cook, stirring often, for 20 to 25 minutes or until the jam gels and the mixture reaches 220°F, measured with a candy thermometer. Test for gel after 20 minutes.

8. Ladle the jam into the headspace to about ¼ inch of the way. Release any present air bubbles using a nonmetallic utensil. Clean the rims and seal with the lids and rings.

9. Process the jars in a hot water bath for 10 minutes. Turn off the heat and let the jars rest in the water bath for 10 minutes.

10. Carefully remove the jars from the hot water canner. Set aside to cool for 12 hours.

11. Check the lids for proper seals. Remove the rings, wipe the jars, label and date them, and transfer to a cupboard or pantry.

12. Refrigerate any jars that don't seal properly, and use within 1 month. Properly

sealed jars will last in the cupboard for 12 months. Once opened, refrigerate and consume within 1 month.

Raspberry Jam

Ingredients

- 2¼ pounds whole fresh red raspberries
- 3½ cups sugar
- ⅓ to ½ cup freshly squeezed lemon juice, as needed

Directions:

1. Prepare a hot water bath. Place the jars in it to keep warm. Wash the lids and rings in hot, soapy water, and set aside.

2. In a preserving pot or a deep pot, combine the raspberries and sugar. With clean hands, a potato masher, or the back of a wooden spoon, mash the berries to release the juices. Taste the mixture and add lemon juice to taste.

3. Bring the mixture to a simmer over medium heat. Reduce the heat to low. Cook for 15 to 20 minutes, stirring often, or until the jam gels and the mixture reaches 220°F, measured with a candy thermometer. Test for gel after 5 minutes.

4. Ladle the jam into the headspace to about ¼ inch of the way. Release any present air bubbles using a nonmetallic utensil. Clean the rims and seal with the lids and rings.

5. Process the jars in a hot water bath for 10 minutes. Turn off the heat and let the jars rest in the water bath for 10 minutes.

6. Carefully remove the jars from the hot water canner. Set aside to cool for 12 hours.

7. Check the lids for proper seals. Remove the rings, wipe the jars, label and date them, and transfer to a cupboard or pantry.

8. Refrigerate any jars that don't seal properly, and use within 2 months. Properly sealed jars will last in the cupboard for 12 months. Once opened, refrigerate and consume within 2 months.

Rosehip Jam

Ingredients

- ½ pound rosehips
- 2 cups red wine
- ¾ cup water
- 1½ cups sugar

Directions:

Days 1 to 3

1. Rinse the rosehips well. Cut the dark spot off the end of each and halve them. Remove the inner seeds and hairs using a small, sturdy spoon.

2. In a large bowl, cover the rosehips with the wine. Refrigerate, covered, for 3 days.

Day 4

1. Prepare a hot water bath. Place the jars in it to keep warm. Wash the lids and rings in hot, soapy water, and set aside.

2. Strain the rosehips.

3. In a small saucepan set over medium-high heat, combine the water and strained rosehips. Cover the pan and bring to a boil. Cook for about 10 minutes, or until the rosehips are tender.

4. Run the rosehips and their cooking water through the fine screen of a food mill.

5. Measure and return the pulp to the saucepan. There should be about 1½ cups of pulp.

6. Add the sugar, adjusting the amount, as needed, to equal the pulp amount.

7. Over medium-high heat, bring the jam to a full, rolling boil. Turn off the heat. Skim off any foam.

8. Ladle the jam into the headspace to about ¼ inch of the way. Release any present air

bubbles using a nonmetallic utensil. Clean the rims and seal with the lids and rings.

9. Process the jars in a hot water bath for 10 minutes. Turn off the heat and let the jars rest in the water bath for 10 minutes.

10. Carefully remove the jars from the hot water canner. Set aside to cool for 12 hours.

11. Check the lids for proper seals. Remove the rings, wipe the jars, label and date them, and transfer to a cupboard or pantry.

12. Refrigerate any jars that don't seal properly, and use within 3 weeks. Properly sealed jars will last in the cupboard for 12 months. Once opened, refrigerate and consume within 3 weeks.

Amazing Pear Mincemeat

Ingredients

- 7 pounds Bartlett pears (around 21 medium)
- 1 lemon
- 2 pounds brilliant or dim raisins
- 6 ¾ cups sugar
- 1 tablespoon cloves
- 1 tablespoon cinnamon
- 1 tablespoon nutmeg
- 1 tablespoon allspice

- 1 teaspoon ginger
- 1 cup vinegar, 5% causticity

Directions

1. PREP: Wash pears and lemon under frosty running water; drain. Sliced pears down the middle the long way and center. Coarsely cleave pears. Cut lemon into quarters and expel seeds finely cleave lemon, including peel, utilizing a food processor or food processor.

2. COOK: Combine all Ingredients in a heavy pan. Heat blend to the point of boiling over medium warmth, mixing to forestall staying. Diminish warmth and stew 30 minutes.

3. FILL: Ladle hot mincemeat into a hot jug, leaving ½ inch headspace. Evacuate air boils. Clean cup edge. Focus top on cup and alter band to fingertip-tight. Place cup on the rack hoisted over stewing water

(180 degrees F) in boiling-water canner. Rehash until all cups are filled.

4. PROCESS: Lower the rack into stewing water. Water must cover cups by 1 inch. Alter warmth to medium-high, cover canner and convey water to a moving boil. Process half quart jugs 25 minutes. Turn off warmth and expel spread. Give shakes a chance to cool 5 minutes. Expel jugs from canner; don't retighten bands assuming free. Cool 12 hours. Test seals. Name and store jugs.

Carrots Canning

Ingredients

- 4-6 lbs carrots (around 24 36 medium 1-to 1/2-inch measurement)
- Salt, optional
- Water
- 6 Pint Ball saving cups with covers and bands

Directions

1. Get ready weight canner. Heat cups in stewing water until prepared for use. Try not to boil. Wash tops in warm lathery water and put bands aside.

2. WASH peel carrots. Wash once more. Cut carrots into cuts or leave entire, slice to fit cups.

3. PACK carrots firmly into hot cups leaving 1 inch headspace. Include 1/2 tsp salt to every 16 ounces cup, if fancied.

4. Spoon boiling water over carrots departing 1 inch headspace. Expel air boils. Wipe edge. Focus hot top on cup. Apply band and conform. Place cup on rack in weight canner containing 2 inches of stewing water. Rehash until all cups are filled.

5. PROCESS half quart cups at 10 pounds weight 25 minutes, as per your canner Method, modifying for elevation. Turn off warmth; cool canner to zero weight. Expel cover following 5 minutes, let cups cool 10

minutes. Expel cups and cool. Check tops for seal following 24 hours. Top ought not to flex all over when focus is squeezed.

Tasty Red Pepper

Ingredients

- 6 lb red ringer peppers (around 14 medium)
- 1 lb Italian plum tomatoes (around 5 medium)
- 2 cloves garlic, unpeeled
- 1 little white onion
- 3/4 cup red wine vinegar

- 2 Tbsp finely cleaved crisp basil
- 1 Tbsp sugar
- 1 tsp salt
- 5 Ball (8 oz) half 16 ounces glass saving jugs with covers and bands

Directions

1. Cook red peppers, tomatoes, garlic and onion under an oven or on a flame broil at 425°F, swinging to dish all sides, until tomatoes and peppers are rankled, darkened and mellowed and garlic and onion are darkened in spots. Expel from warmth.

2. PLACE pepper and tomatoes in paper packs, secure opening and let cool around 15 minutes. Permit garlic and onion to cool. Peel garlic and onion. Finely slash garlic. Put aside. Finely hack onion, measuring 1/4 cup. Put aside. Peel and seed peppers and tomatoes. Place peppers and tomatoes in a food processor or blender,

working in bunches, and process until smooth.

3. Get ready boiling water canner. Heat jugs in stewing water until prepared for use. Try not to boil. Wash covers in warm foamy water and put bands aside.

4. Join pepper and tomato puree, garlic, onion, vinegar, basil, sugar and salt in a huge pot. Heat to the point of boiling. Decrease warmth and stew until blend thickens and hills on a spoon, around 20 minutes.

5. Scoop hot spread into hot cups leaving 1/2 inch headspace. Wipe edge. Focus hot cover on cup.

6. Expel jugs and cool. Check tops for seal following 24 hours. Cover ought not to flex here and there when focus is squeezed.

Healthy Grape Jelly

Ingredients

- 3 cups locally acquired, unsweetened grape juice
- 4 Tbsp Ball RealFruit Classic Pectin
- 1/2 tsp spread or margarine
- 1/2 cups granulated sugar

Directions

1. MEASURE 3 cups grape juice in a 4-cup or bigger fluid measuring cup. Bit by bit whisk pectin into juice until completely fused. (Pectin won't be totally broken down right now.) Pour juice blend into the

perfect Pot fitted with the Stirrer. Include spread/margarine to diminish frothing.

2. PRESS jam catch – the cook time will naturally default to 25 minutes. Press enter.

3. Sit tight 4 minutes for machine to sound 4 short beeps demonstrating that the time has come to include sugar. Include sugar continuously while Stirrer keeps running.

4. THE APPLIANCE will keep on automatically blend your Ingredients while it cooks. Stay inside earshot of the Jam and Jelly Maker, the apparatus will beep again toward the end of the procedure flagging jam cooking is finished. Press drop and unplug the machine.

5. Evacuate Stirrer utilizing a pot holder. Skim froth, if important, from top of jam.

6. Save grape jam quickly, utilizing 1 of the 3 routes recorded here.

Canned Chicken

Ingredients:

- 18 medium boneless and skinless chicken breasts
- 1 ½ tablespoons of salt
- 4 ½ cups of water
- Butter or Olive Oil for frying in skillet

Directions:

1. Cook each side of the chicken in a skillet with some butter or olive oil, about 8-10 minutes. Remove from heat when the chicken is white and cooked all the way through. If you poke it with a fork, the juices run clear.

2. In each pint jar place a ½ teaspoon of salt and 2 chicken breasts.

3. Fill the jar with water, process for 70 minutes at 10 pounds of pressure for the weighted gauge of the pressure canner or 11 pounds if the pressure canner has a dial gauge.

4. Remove jars, and let cool until it is room temperature, which may take about a day.

Mexican Turkey Soup

Ingredients:

- 6 cups of cooked turkey, chopped
- 2 cups of chopped onions
- 8 ounces can of Mexican green chilies, chopped and drained
- ¼ cup of taco seasoning mix, packed
- 28 ounces of crushed tomatoes with the juices
- 16 cups of turkey or chicken broth
- 3 cups of corn
- 1 ½ tablespoons of extra virgin olive oil

Directions:

1. In a large stockpot, warm olive oil on medium-high heat. Sauté the onions until tender and fragrant, about 2 minutes on

medium-high heat. Reduce heat to medium-low.

2. Add taco seasoning and the chilies. Cook and stir for another 3 minutes, add in the tomatoes and the broth. Bring to a boil, and then add the corn and the turkey.

3. Reduce heat to low, and let simmer for 10 minutes.

4. Ladle equally into the jars.

5. Process pints at 10 pounds for 75 minutes and quarts at 10 pounds for 90 minutes for the weighted gauge of the pressure canner or 11 pounds if the pressure canner has a dial gauge.

6. Remove jars, and let cool until it is at room temperature. This may take about a day.

Fish

Ingredients:

- 5 pounds tuna or salmon
- 5 pint sized mason jars with lids and rings
- Canning salt

- Lemon juice
- 1 jalapeño pepper

Directions:

1. Place 1 slice of jalapeño pepper into each jar.

2. Fill jars with meat to 1/2 inch from the top.

3. Add 1/4 tsp. canning salt and 1 tsp. lemon juice per pint.

4. Use a knife to jiggle meat and remove any air pockets.

5. Wipe rim of jar clean.

6. Heat lids in hot water for 3 minutes; place lids on jars and tighten rings slightly.

7. Place jars in canner and fill with water to the jar rings.

8. Close and lock pressure canner and bring to a boil over high heat, then add cooking weight to the top.

9. After 20 minutes, turn heat to medium and cook for 75 minutes. Turn off heat and

leave canner alone until it has cooled completely to room temperature.

10. After canner has cooled, remove jars from the canner and check for sealing.

11. If jars have sealed, store for up to 2 years; if not, use meat right away.

Cabbage Soup

Ingredients:

- 2 kg of minced meat
- 1 large onion, diced
- 2 garlic cloves, minced
- 6 cups of cabbage, grated
- 1 cup diced celery
- 1 cup diced green pepper
- 2 cans of light beans (16 ounces)
- 8 glasses of canned tomatoes with juice (2 liters if you can make your own 7like me)

- 10 cubes of veal broth
- 8 cups of water
- 2 tablespoons of garlic powder
- 20 rounds of fresh pepper corn (I use it)
- 2 teaspoons of sea salt
- 1 tablespoon of dried parsley
- 2 tablespoons of dried basil
- 1 tablespoon of thyme
- 1 teaspoon dried celery

Directions:

Sterilizing

Sterilize to prepare glass jars, lids and rings. Chop and cut all the vegetables and set aside. Collect all the dry ingredients and set them aside

Cooking:

1. Minced meat: brown minced meat in a pan so far pink. Separate 3 tablespoons of onion and garlic fat. If desired, drain and wash the meat to remove excess oil.

2. Prepare the beef: heat 8 cups of water in a large bowl, or use 2-liter jars filled with water in each jar - 5 cubes of beef broth.

3. Microwave for 5 minutes to dissolve the cubes. Remove it carefully, it will be very hot, stir quickly to make sure the cubes are thawed.

4. Sautéed onion and garlic: pour 3 tablespoons of fat in a large saucepan and wrap the chopped onions and fry the garlic until tender.

5. Mix with other ingredients: add cooked minced meat, cabbage, celery, green pepper, beans, fruit juice, tomato and broth - mix well.

6. Mix all the dry ingredients: garlic powder, pepper, sea salt, parsley, basil, thyme and celery. Boil, and cook for 20 minutes. Actually your soup is ready to eat at this point.

Filling jars:

Note: protect the counter by using a cloth or towel to adjust the jars since you will fill the hot jars.

Make use of a spoon strainer to fill the jars with half-filled solids, then fill the rest of the jar with water up to 1 inch in the cavity. Using a clean, damp cloth, remove any particles or water from the edge of the glass jar, insert the lid and ring and squeeze with your finger. When filling each can, place it in the pressure container. Make sure to place the shelf under the can.

Processing:

Place the lid on the box and lock it. Set the temperature to high. Vent the steam for it

Beef Stew

Ingredients:

- 2 tablespoons extra-virgin olive oil, divided
- 5 pounds stew beef, cut into bite-size pieces
- 10 cups potatoes, peeled and cubed
- 8 cups medium carrots, peeled and chopped
- 3 cups chopped onions

- 2 cups chopped celery
- 6 medium Roma tomatoes, diced (3 cups)
- 4½ teaspoons coarse sea salt (optional)
- 1 tablespoon dried parsley
- 1 tablespoon dried oregano
- ½ tablespoon celery seeds
- 1 teaspoon ground coriander
- 1 teaspoon dried thyme
- 1 teaspoon dried basil
- ½ teaspoon ground black pepper
- 8 cups Beef Broth
- 5 cups water

Directions:

1. In a thick-bottomed stockpot, heat 1 tablespoon oil and brown the beef in batches until all the beef is lightly browned, about 3 to 5 minutes per batch. Add 1 additional tablespoon of oil while browning each batch. Remove each batch

from the stockpot and place in a bowl. Be sure not to fully cook the beef.

2. Return the browned beef to the stockpot and add the potatoes, carrots, onions, celery, tomatoes, salt (if using), parsley, oregano, celery seeds, coriander, thyme, basil, and pepper and mix well. Add the Beef Broth and water and mix well. Bring to a boil over medium-high heat, stirring frequently. Boil for 5 minutes then remove from the heat.

3. Ladle the hot stew into hot jars, leaving 1 inch of headspace. Remove any air bubbles and add additional stew if necessary to maintain the 1 inch of headspace.

4. Wipe the rim of each jar with a warm washcloth dipped in distilled white vinegar. Place a lid and ring on each jar and hand tighten.

5. Place jars in the pressure canner, lock the pressure canner lid, and bring to a boil on high heat. Let the canner vent for 10 minutes. Close the vent and continue heating to achieve 11 PSI for a dial gauge and 10 PSI for a weighted gauge. Process

quart jars for 1 hour 30 minutes and pint jars for 1 hour 15 minutes.

INGREDIENT TIP: Using a pressure canner makes even the toughest cuts of meat tender and flavorful. Beef sold for stew typically comes from chuck or round roasts, cut into 1½-inch pieces. Bottom and eye cuts, also known as round, are typically leaner than a chuck roast, which are cuts from the shoulder, leg, and butt. When cutting into bite-size pieces, cut to a size you would feel comfortable seeing on the end of your fork or spoon.

Potato and Leek Soup

Ingredients:

- 6 potatoes, peeled and cubed
- 4 cups stock, chicken or beef
- 5 pounds leeks, washed and cut into ¼-inch slices

Directions:

1. Layer leaks in the bottom of each jar. Place a layer of potatoes on top of the leeks, followed by another layer of the sliced leaks.

2. Boil the chicken or beef stock before pouring into the jars. Make sure to leave about an inch of space at the top of each jar.

3. Attach the lids to the jars and process in a pressure canner using 11 pounds for 60 minutes.

Veggie Soup

Ingredients:

- 6 cups tomatoes (cored, peeled, chopped)
- 2 cups tomatillos (chopped)
- 1 cup onion (chopped)
- 1 cup carrots (chopped)
- 1 cup green bell pepper (chopped)
- 1 cup red bell pepper (chopped)

- 6 cups corn kernels
- ½ cup hot pepper (seeded, chopped)
- 1 teaspoon cayenne pepper
- **5 cups tomato juice**
- 1 tablespoon hot sauce
- 2 teaspoon chili powder
- 2 teaspoon cumin (ground)
- **1 teaspoon salt**
- **2 cups water**
- 1 teaspoon black pepper

Directions:

Sterilize the jars.

1. Combine all the ingredients in a pot and bring to boil.
2. Simmer uncovered for 15 minutes on low flame.
3. Distribute the solids and liquid among the jars, leaving one-inch of headspace.

4. Get rid of any air bubbles and clean the rims.

5. Cover the jars with the lid and apply the bands making sure that it is tightened.

6. Process the jars for 60 minutes at 10 pounds pressure in a pressure canner.

7. Remove; allow cooling, and then labeling the jars.

Fennel & Carrot Soup

Ingredients:

- 1 lb. fennel bulbs (trimmed)
- 1 tablespoon olive oil
- 4 ½ lbs. carrots (peeled, sliced)
- 12 cups vegetable stock
- 2 teaspoon onion powder
- 2 tablespoon salt
- 1 teaspoon dried ginger (ground)
- 1 teaspoon dried thyme

- ½ teaspoon cumin (ground)
- 3 tablespoon lemon juice
- 1 teaspoon black pepper (ground)
- 1 teaspoon dried coriander (ground)

Directions:

1. Sterilize the jars.
2. Heat oil in a pot and sauté the fennel in it till translucent.
3. Mix in the carrots and 4 cups vegetable broth and simmer for 30 minutes.
4. Leave to cool, and then puree the mixture.
5. Return to the pot and mix in the remainder of the ingredients.
6. Bring to boil and simmer for 20-30 minutes.
7. Ladle the mix immediately into the sterilized jars, leaving one-inch of headspace.
8. Get rid of any air bubbles and clean the rims.

9. Cover the jars with the lid and apply the bands making sure that it is tightened.

10. Process the jars for 35 minutes at 10 pounds pressure in a pressure canner.

11. Remove; allow cooling, and then labeling the jars.

Tomato Soup

Ingredients:

- 15 lbs. tomatoes (chopped roughly)
- 2 tablespoon olive oil
- 3 cups celery (chopped)
- 3 cups onions (chopped)
- 1 tablespoon salt
- 1 tablespoon pepper
- 64 oz. vegetable stock
- ¼ cup garlic (chopped)
- 32 oz. water
- 2 cups carrots (chopped)

Directions:

1. Sterilize the jars.
2. Heat olive oil in a pot and sauté the onions, celery and carrots in it.
3. Mix in the tomatoes, salt, pepper, stock and water and leave to simmer for 2 hours.
4. Pour the soup using an immersion blender.
5. Ladle the mix immediately into the sterilized jars, leaving one-inch of headspace.
6. Get rid of any air bubbles and clean the rims.
7. Cover the jars with the lid and apply the bands making sure that it is tightened.
8. Submerge the jars within a prepared boiling water canner and leave to process for 20 minutes.
9. Remove; allow cooling, and then labeling the jars.

Chicken Soup

Ingredients:

- 3 cups chicken (diced)
- 6 cups chicken broth
- 10 cups water
- 1 cup onion (diced)
- Salt and pepper to taste
- 1 ½ cups celery (diced)
- 1 ½ cups carrots (sliced)
- 3 chicken bouillon cubes

Directions:

1. Sterilize the jars.
2. Combine all the ingredients in a pot except the salt, pepper and bouillon cubes and bring to boil.
3. Reduce the flame and simmer for 30 minutes.
4. Stir in the remaining ingredients and stir cook until the bouillon cubes dissolve.

5. Turn-off the flame and skim-off any visible foam.

6. Ladle the mix immediately into the sterilized jars, leaving one-inch of headspace.

7. Get rid of any air bubbles and clean the rims.

8. Cover the jars with the lid and apply the bands making sure that it is tightened.

9. Process the jars for 1 hour 15 minutes at 10 pounds pressure in a pressure canner.

10. Remove; allow cooling, and then labeling the jars.

Home-style Spaghetti Sauce

Ingredients

- 2 lbs. ground beef
- 4 cups chopped onion
- 16 oz. tomato sauce
- 24 oz. tomato paste
- 4 tsp. pepper
- 4 tsps. dried parsley
- 4 tsps. dried basil
- 4 tbsps. brown sugar
- 4 tsps. salt

- 8 cups water
- 2 bay leaves

Directions

1. Place a large saucepot over medium-high heat. Boil ground beef with onion until all pink disappears. Reduce heat; add tomato paste, tomato sauce, pepper, and every other ingredient. Stirring frequently, boil for 45 minutes.

2. Ladle hot sauce into each canning jar. Remember to leave one-inch headspace. Use spatula to remove air bubbles, then use a clean cloth to wipe jar rims, after that, adjust lids, and screw band.

3. Set the filled jars in a pressure canner at 11 pounds pressure for dial-gauge or 10 pounds for the weighted-gauge canner. Process heat jars for twenty minutes, adjusting for altitude. Switch off the heat and let pressure drop naturally. Remove the lid and cool the jars in canner for five minutes. Take out the jars and cool. Inspect lids seal after twenty-four hours.

Tomato Soup with Celery

Ingredients

- 6 medium onions, sliced
- 1 bunch celery, sliced
- 5-quarts tomato juice or 8-quarts fresh chopped tomatoes
- 1 cup of sugar
- 1/4 cup of salt
- 1 cup butter
- 1 cup flour

Directions:

1. Add chopped celery and onions in a large pot with a little amount of water to prevent them from burning. Place pot over medium heat. Bring to boil. While boiling, add tomatoes to the pot and cook to become softened. Place the combination all through a strainer. And then return to pot. Add salt and sugar.

2. Combine flour and butter. Mix well and add 2 cups of cold juice until well blend. Add flour and butter mixture to warm juice (before it is hot to prevent flour lumps). Stir well. The flour can turn lumpy if it reaches a boil, so only heat to hot and turn off the heater before boiling - It would keep thickening as it cools.

3. Ladle hot soup into each canning jar. Remember to leave one-inch headspace. Use spatula to remove air bubbles, then use a clean cloth to wipe jar rims, after that, adjust lids, and screw band.

4. Set the filled jars in a pressure canner at 11 pounds pressure for dial-gauge or 10 pounds for the weighted-gauge canner.

Process heat jars for twenty-five minutes, adjusting for altitude. Switch off heat and let pressure drop naturally. Remove the lid and cool the jars in the canner for three minutes. Take out the jars and cool. Inspect lids seal after twenty-four hours.

Carrot, Coriander, and Ginger Soup

Ingredients:

- 1 big onion, chopped

- 3 tbsps butter

- 2 whole cloves peeled garlic

- 3 pounds carrots, chopped

- 2 ribs celery, chopped

- 3 tbsps. fresh ginger, chopped
- 8 cups vegetable or chicken broth
- 1 tsp. ground coriander
- 1/2 cup honey
- 1 tsp. ground ginger
- Fresh ground black pepper and salt

Directions

1. Melt the butter in a large saucepot over medium-high heat. Add onion, garlic, carrot, ginger root, and celery to butter and cook for 10 minutes with frequent stirring.

2. Add the broth to the veggies and allow it to boil. Reduce heat and leave to cook for about 30 minutes so the carrots are tender.

3. Take it out of heat sauce. Add ground ginger, honey, and coriander. Puree the soup in the pot either in batches with a regular blender or using an immersion blender.

4. Ladle the hot soup into each canning jar. Remember to leave one-inch headspace.

Use spatula to remove air bubbles, then use a clean cloth to wipe jar rims, after that, adjust lids, and screw band.

5. Set the filled jars in a pressure canner at eleven pounds pressure for dial-gauge or ten pounds for the weighted-gauge canner. Process heat jars for seven-five minutes, adjusting for altitude. Switch off the heat and let pressure drop naturally. Remove the lid and cool the jars in canner for five minutes. Take out the jars and cool. Inspect lids for seal after twenty-four hours.

6. To serve: Add a less than 1/2 a cup of heavy cream to each one-liter jar. Reheat a jar and stir so all ingredients are well-blend. Add seasoning to taste and serve.

Singapore Pepper Sauce

Ingredients:

- 4 cups fresh hot red peppers, seeded and chopped
- 2-1/2 cup granulated sugar
- White vinegar, 5 % acidity
- 1-1/2 cup rinsed sultana raisins
- 1 tbsps. grated fresh ginger root
- 1/4 cup chopped garlic
- 2 tsps. salt

Directions:

1. Combine sugar and vinegar in a large saucepot and place over medium-high heat. Bring to boil, stirring intermittently. Reduce heat and leave to boil for three minutes.

2. Add gingerroot, garlic, red pepper, sultanas, and salt. Allow it to boil for five minutes. Remove from the sauce of heat.

3. Ladle hot sauce into each canning jar. Remember to leave one-inch headspace. Use spatula to remove air bubbles, then use a clean cloth to wipe jar rims, after that, adjust lids, and screw band.

4. Set the filled jars in a pressure canner at eleven pounds pressure for dial-gauge or ten pounds for the weighted-gauge canner Process heat jars for ten minutes, adjusting for altitude. Switch off the heat and let pressure drop naturally. Remove the lid and cool the jars in canner for five minutes. Take out the jars and cool. Inspect lids for seal after twenty-four hours

Green Lima Vegetable Soup

Ingredients

- 4 cups sliced, peeled, cored tomatoes (approx. 6 medium)

- 3 cups 3/4 inch chopped carrots (approx.. 6 medium)

- 3 cups peeled and cubed potatoes (approx.. 3 medium)

- 2 cups corn kernels, uncooked (approx. 4-1/2 ears)

- 2 cups green lima beans (approx. 3/4 lb.)

- 1 cup sliced onions (1 medium)

- 1 cup 1-inch chopped celery (around 2 stalks)
- Pepper, optional
- Salt, optional
- 3 cups of water

Directions:

1. In a medium saucepot, combine all the vegetables. Pour water and allow it to boil. Reduce the heat and cook for five minutes. Add pepper and salt if you wish.

2. Ladle hot veggie soup into each canning jar. Remember to leave one-inch headspace. Use spatula to remove air bubbles, then use a clean cloth to wipe jar rims, after that, adjust lids, and screw band.

3. Set the filled jars in a pressure canner at 11 pounds pressure for dial-gauge or 10 pounds for the weighted-gauge canner. Process heat jars for fifty-five minutes, adjusting for altitude. Switch off the heat and let pressure come down naturally. Remove the lid and cool the jars in the canner for ten minutes. Take out the jars

and cool. Inspect lids seal after about twenty-four hours.

Cabbage and Corned Beef Soup

Ingredients

- 1 large onion, sliced
- 1-1/2 cup sliced carrot
- 1-1/2 cup chopped celery
- 1-1/2 can tomato sauce or juice
- 1/3 tsp. ground allspice
- 5 cups beef stock
- 2 cups potatoes cut into 1/2 inch dices
- 1 small head cabbage, sliced

- 1/2 lb. corned beef, diced into 1/2 cubes, trim fat
- 1/2 tsp. black pepper
- 1 tsp. canning salt
- 2 cups water

Directions

1. Layer equal quantities of carrots, onions, celery, cabbage, corned beef, and potatoes to each cleaned canning jars to around ¾ full.

2. In a medium saucepot, add tomato sauce or juice, beef stock, allspice, pepper, salt, and water. Allow it to boil and remove from the heat source.

3. Ladle the mixture into each canning jar Remember to leave one-inch headspace. If necessary, add more hot water or stock each canning jar. Use spatula to remove air bubbles, then use a clean cloth to wipe jar rims, after that, adjust lids, and screw band.

4. Set the filled jars in a pressure canner at 11 pounds pressure for dial-gauge or 10

pounds for the weighted-gauge canner. Process heat jars for seventy-five minutes, adjusting for altitude. Switch off the heat and let pressure drop naturally. Remove the lid and cool the jars in canner for five minutes. Take out the jars and cool. Inspect lids seal after twenty-four hours

Chicken Broth with Chile and Corn

Ingredients

- 2 tbsps. veggies oil

- 1 cup sliced celery (about 2 stalks)

- 1-1/2 sliced onions, (about 3 medium)

- 2 poblano chile pepper, seeded and sliced

- 2 tsps. mild chili powder or ground chile peppers
- 12 cups chicken stock
- 4 cups sliced chicken, cooked
- 5 cups freshly picked corn kernels
- 1/2 tsp. black pepper, freshly ground
- Slices of American cheese
- instantly crushed potato flakes

Directions

1. Heat the oil over medium-high heat in a large saucepot. Add celery, onions, and chiles, cook and stir for five minutes or until softened. Add chili powder, stirring frequently, cook for one minute.

2. Add chopped chicken, stock, corn, and black pepper. Allow it to boil.

3. Ladle vegetables and chicken into each canning jar by filling halfway and add broth. Remember to leave one-inch headspace. Use spatula to remove air

bubbles, then use a clean cloth to wipe jar rims, after that, adjust lids, and screw band.

4. Set the filled jars in a pressure canner at eleven pounds pressure for dial-gauge or ten pounds for the weighted-gauge canner. Process heat jars for seven-five minutes, adjusting for altitude. Switch off the heat and let pressure drop naturally. Remove the lid and cool the jars in canner for five minutes. Take out the jars and cool. Inspect lids for seal after twenty-four hours.

5. To serve, in a medium saucepot, add contents of one jar. Bring to a boil. Simmer, covered ten minutes. Take the pot out of the heat. Add 3/4-ounce slices American cheese and 1/2 cup instant crushed potato flakes torn, to soup, stir thoroughly to melt cheese.

Tasty Beef & Vegetables

Ingredients

- 3 pounds hamburger
- 6 cups frozen peas
- 5 pounds red skin potatoes, diced large
- 1 large red onion, cubed
- 6 tbsps. minced garlic
- 6 tbsps. steak seasoning

- Pepper and Salt to taste
- 6 cups beef stock
- 6 cups water

Directions:

1. Place a large saucepot over medium-high heat. Add burger and season with pepper and salt. Stir and smash burger into bits as it turns brown. Drain fat and place back browned meat to saucepot. Put to one side.

2. Ladle browned meat half-full into each canning the jar. Pack meat down into the jars. Add 1 cup of frozen peas and 1 tbsp of minced garlic to each jar. Ladle in potatoes to fill the remaining space, leaving 1¼ inch headspace. Thrust the potatoes with your fingers so that it can contain more of it. Add ¼ cup of red onions and 1 tbsp of steak seasoning of your choice to each jar.

3. Add a cup of beef stock and a cup of water to each jar until water leveled with potatoes. Remember to leave one-inch headspace. Use spatula to remove air

bubbles, then use a clean cloth to wipe jar rims, after that, adjust lids, and screw band.

4. Set the filled jars in a pressure canner at 11 pounds pressure for dial-gauge or 10 pounds for the weighted-gauge canner. Process heat jars for ninety minutes, adjusting for altitude. Switch off the heat and let pressure drop naturally. Remove the lid and cool the jars in canner for five minutes. Take out the jars and cool. Inspect lids seal after twenty-four hours.

Mexican Chicken Soup

Ingredients

- 1 large boneless chicken breast (boiled, cubed or shredded)
- 1/4 cup chopped carrots
- 2/3 Cup chopped celery
- 1 medium onion, sliced
- 2/3 can of tomatoes
- 2/3 can of kidney beans
- 1 cup cubed tomatoes

- 2 cups chicken stock
- 2 cups water
- 1 cup corn (fresh or frozen)
- 1 garlic cloves (crushed)
- 1/3 tsp. ground cumin
- 1/3 tbsp. canning salt
- 1 chicken bouillon cube

Directions

1. Combine all ingredients in a large saucepot. Place over medium-heat heat and bring to a boil, cover and boil for three minutes. Reduce heat and chicken, cook slowly for five minutes.

2. Ladle hot soup into canning jars. Remember to leave one-inch headspace. Use spatula to remove air bubbles, then use a clean cloth to wipe jar rims, after that, adjust lids, and screw band.

3. Set the filled jars in a pressure canner at 11 pounds pressure for dial-gauge or 10 pounds for the weighted-gauge canner.

Process heat jars for 75 minutes, adjusting for altitude. Switch off the heat and let pressure drop naturally. Remove the lid and cool the jars in canner for 5 minutes. Take out the jars and cool. Inspect lids seal after twenty-four hours

Chapter 6: Frequently asked questions

When packing jars, is the headspace really important?

Yes, leaving the stated amount of headspace in a jar allows a vacuum seal during processing. If too little headspace, the food may expand and bubble out when air is being forced out from under the lid. The bubbling food can leave a deposit on the seal of the lid or the jar's rim and prevent the jar from sealing properly. If too much headspace, jars may not seal and the food at the top is likely to discolor.

How long can canned food be stored?

Properly preserved food stored in a dry, cool place will retain optimum eating quality for at least one year. Canned food stored in a warm place in indirect sunlight, near a furnace, hot pipes, or a range may lose some of its eating quality in a few weeks or months, depending on the temperature.

Is it safe to use the oven for food processing?

No. This can be dangerous as the temperature will vary depending on the accuracy of the oven regulators and the heat circulation. Dry heat penetrates into jars of food very slowly. Jars can also easily explode in the oven.

Why do you need to exhaust a pressure canner?

If the pot is not exhausted, the temperature inside may not match the pressure on the gauge. Before closing the valve, the steam should be allowed to escape for 10 minutes.

Should liquid lost during processing be replaced?

No. Loss of liquid does not cause spoilage of the food, although food above the liquid may become darker.

Is it all right to reuse jar bands and lids?

Screw bands can be reused unless they are badly rusted or the top edge is pried up that would prevent a proper seal. Lids should never be reused since the sealing compound becomes indented by the first usage, preventing another airtight seal.

Is it safe to use the canning method of an open kettle?

No. This method means that food is cooked in a usual kettle (an open pot), then packed into hot jars and sealed without processing. The temperatures obtained are not hot enough to destroy all the dangerous microorganisms in the food. Contamination may also occur when transferring food from the kettle to the jars.

What causes the undersides of jar lids to discolor?

Natural compounds in some products, particularly acids, corrode metal and cause dark deposits on the underside of jar lids. This deposit is harmless providing the contents have been properly processed and the jar has a good seal.

Why do jars break down during processing?

Canning jars will break down for several reasons:

Putting jars of unheated or raw food directly into boiling water in the canner. This rapid change of temperature is too high and will crack jars.

Using commercial food jars

Putting hot food in cold jars

Using jars that have chips or cracks

Jars bumping against each other during canning

Placing jars directly on the bottom of canner instead of on a rack

Can hard water scale or film be removed from canning jars?

This can be often be accomplished by soaking jars for several hours in a solution of 1 gallon of water + 1 cup vinegar.

Questions About Canning Fruits and Vegetables

Is it safe to preserve food without salt?

Yes. Salt is only used for flavor and is not necessary to prevent spoilage.

Is it safe to preserve fruits without sugar?

Yes. Sugar is added to retain the shape of the fruit, improve flavor, and help stabilize color. It is not added as a preservative.

If aspirin is used, can vegetables and fruits be canned without heating?

No. Aspirin should not be used for preservation. It cannot be relied on to give satisfactory products or to prevent spoilage. Adequate heat treatment is the only safe procedure.

If vinegar is used, is it safe to can green beans in a boiling water bath?

No. Do not shorten recommended processing times if vinegar is used for preserving fresh vegetables (this does not refer to pickled vegetables).

Should I precook all vegetables before canning?

For best quality, yes. However, some vegetables can be packed cold or raw into jars before being processed in the pressure canner.

What vegetables expand rather than shrink during processing?

Lima beans, corn, and peas are starchy and expand during processing. They should be packed loosely.

What makes corn turn brown during canning?

Most often this occurs when too high a temperature is used, causing caramelization of the sugar in the corn. Also because of some minerals in the water used in canning.

Questions about Canning Meats

Is it safe to can poultry and meat without salt?

Yes. Salt is used only for flavoring and is not necessary for safe processing.

Should chicken giblets be canned in the same jar with chicken?

No. Their flavor may penetrate other pieces of chicken in the jar.

Chapter 7: Some Other Food Preservation Techniques

The Milling Technique

The ancient humans found out that by crushing different berries and wheat kernels by placing them in between two pieces of rocks they can get flour, which can be used in a variety of different forms. Since that time grinding flour with the help of various techniques has been part of human civilization.

Milling is used as the easiest way of getting the fullest nutrient content from wheat flour. This method is the demand of modern day as the shelf life of flour needs to be increased as food is supplied from one part of the world to the other. For this reason, the removal of all sorts of grain bran traces and germs is highly essential. Milling as a procedure will enable the user to get the required amount of flour every time so that it can be consumed within a time period of 72 hours.

Why go for milling:

The flour grains consist of around 90% of minerals, vitamins, and protein which are needed by the human body. But in the case of commercially milled flour, the quantity of these nutrients is largely reduced because of artificial additives and processing.

The whole grain comprises of three major parts, two being the germ and the bran. These two hold all of the minerals, vitamins and proteins. On the other hand, when milled, the oils present in the germ and bran starts oxidizing. So eventually, the flour turns rancid within a period of 72 hours. So the commercial packaging of flour removes all bran and of germ and thus all the connected nutrients, which elongates the shelf life. In Commercially processed flour you will get only the third ingredient of the grain, called endosperm. It is the starchy center, which is white in color and no useful nutrients are present in it.

Methods Applied

If you are also curious about the quality of food you eat and especially the most frequently used eatable, i.e. flour. You need to be curious about this method of food processing.

Various methods of milling are applied, some of which include:

Manual Milling

This allows manual milling of Grain, in which a mill which is operated by hand is applied. Although time-consuming yet this method is quite cost friendly.

Electric Milling

As compared to manual method electric milling is fast in which mill is supplied with a power connection. If you have to mill large quantities of flour, then this method is the most suitable one.

Motorized Milling

Flour can also be milled in a way which is partially supported by the machines. In this methods, the mill is connected to an electric or gas motor along a pulley system. This method is faster than manual milling but slower than the electric milling process.

The equipment used for various types of mills is as follows:

In the case of the stone mill is a set of two grinding stones which are circular in shape. One stein is kept stationary while the other one is moved against it.

In the case of burr mill, the grinding wheels of the wheel are made up of steel with tiny burrs extending from the sides.

In the case of impact mill, the major assembly is just like the stone mill but various rows of blades are used to circular rows.

Conclusion

Canning is related to preservation of food on your own. In this modern era, it is no less than a blessing. Although the basic necessity of food remains the same for all human generations yet the ways in which this need is fulfilled have changed. Today you will get food with plenty of addition like additives, hormones, chemical sprays and steroids. When one is canning and preserving at his own, one of the best benefits is to know about the actual chemical composition of the food. Ultimately the health of all those, who consume this natural form of food is preserved and taken care of.

Once you get the hang of canning your own food, you will be unstoppable! I will not lie to you and tell you that everything will be easy – especially the first couple of times. You will make a couple of mistakes and you might make a mess of your kitchen too. This is expected – you are a beginner after all.

As time goes by, though, the number of mistakes you make will decrease and eventually, you won't need this guide to assist you. You will be able to come up with creative recipes of your own! This all has to start with the first steps, the first steps being your giving this a chance.

If you aren't feeling confident in your abilities, try out the easiest water bath canning recipe in this book.

Don't let your fears stop you from trying out this great method of preserving your own food. It is a highly rewarding experience that is capable of benefitting you for years to come.

You won't regret trying it out.

© written by : Elisa Dayson

www.ingramcontent.com/pod-product-compliance
Lightning Source LLC
Chambersburg PA
CBHW070658120526
44590CB00013BA/1008